A
STOIC
DOCTRINE

A
STOIC
DOCTRINE

Reason and Faith

S C R I P T

iUniverse, Inc.
Bloomington

A STOIC DOCTRINE
Reason and Faith

iUniverse books may be ordered through booksellers or by contacting:

iUniverse
1663 Liberty Drive
Bloomington, IN 47403
www.iuniverse.com
1-800-Authors (1-800-288-4677)

ISBN: 978-1-4697-9243-9 (sc)
ISBN: 978-1-4697-9293-4 (ebk)

Printed in the United States of America

iUniverse rev. date: 02/24/2012

No matter the cause, no matter the incongruent, we must step aside and realize life is here for us and not the other way around. Sure I love life but does that mean I have to live in it, Yes, but why must I live with the unfaithful, with the unbelievable, and the incongruent in logic that life is here for the main cause that we love being nothing?

Does life really matter? Do we hate or love for the good of everyone? Is anything worth our time and reality? Are we so not conscious, and without awareness, sensation, or cognition of the utmost or exceedingly great in degree in self interest of an act of that something exists, or is true that no way dictates our lives to what is agreeable to reason or sound judgment? Do we love but only in loving have a disagreement with an existence in, or formed by an existence to go on or keep on, as in some course or action, or lasting in permanently forever in the idea that love is unconditional? Can I not live but only in living hate that which I do not like because of an absence of comfort or ease, or not easy in body or mind, in causing discomfort or distress, painful, irritating, restless, disturbed, perturbed, or pain in utter state of great commotion, confusion, or disturbance, and tumult, and agitation, and lack of calm, peace, or ease, and anxiety, and uneasiness?

What will we do to revive or restore after neglect or a period of forgetting if even in our natural existence we have no care for anyone such that it matters not in a careful and particular way?

Can we really love but only in love hate that is which is unreal? How about are we to love or hate or be so considered or include as part of something more to carry, bringing, or taking from one place to another (metaphorically), or involving in one state or quality of becoming external and being self to revoked, or to withdraw formally or officially and to connect sanity, and bring into relational thoughts, memories, actions, or reasons that associates to defer out terms that we are to renounce a cause and calling? Also, is there a right in power to claim with responsibility in a formal manner tending to correct or rectify the science of reason in honor and truth? Now, why would we not want more but only in wanting have more to give than to receive, and lay open to something's specified such that myself as a person or a thing of individual character or a distinguishing feature of myself or quality to correspond exactly, as in nature, with my own characteristic in my mind for you to understand deeper meaning in colloquial ways of life's mysteries? Maybe so, I do not know, but let me continue.

How would we not love and in finding that we do not want more? Why must we be so deeply interested and involved to extend the act of abandoning something in ourselves or something we love in acting or serving in place of another individual in a process, or an act of person in their reasoning with the appearance of their mind, or eye that will give no forthright attitude to draw out to the length of a cause, and have a supreme or astounding life of goodness and reason as all life should have it with directing you or me to the ultimate deniability that God is greater than us?

The Hatefulness of Fatherhood

Does a son like his father for the basis or ground work of anything in relation to cause and effect for lacking power, and ability in knowledge, and that the right to stretch out one's being be considered to be good or respectable through a usage that is influential in being congruent towards ones equality, as in amount, status, or character as God would have it?

God Grants Teaching to those who have learned

And just exactly how are we to love by a mere product of mental activity or instance of creating or producing by exercise of the imagination, in listening to a father who has or never will care that our existences are to envy or resent the pleasure or good fortune of ourselves in causing fear, suspicion or fear of future trouble or evil, or to fear greatly to regard from resulting from a specified cause or reason, and yes this is very respectable for, for why would it not be except to protect the child?! This state of being throws me for a loop when I am looking at an arrangement that is accepted by both individuals to a **transaction,** and a publishing of accounts that show proceedings, as papers are read, addresses delivered, or discussed, as say a meeting where an ample supply of individuals who know of love or the like come together with states or quality of being real with each other to form notions, opinions, or purposes in having completed, and adamantly revised unlimited knowledge, awareness, or understanding in perspiring tough love? Perceiving this for a child and parent is essential in all things that are directing the universe and the affairs of humankind with the wise desire to do good to others, and find good occurrences or complement's as well as substitutes, and reserves of substitutes in likeability cause a need for action that it must be perceived in many languages and refers to the participation in the action or state of action. So, what I am speaking of is the verbal form of using adequate knowledge and science as an adjective proceeds in not standing alone but in an effective manner with a sentence in being peaceable, and free from wrongs, and pangs but gives the expression as the Stoic's would have it: "Free from passions and pleasures but only needing them in moderation."

Although, thinking in this manner does not specify who we are as a person or where our position is in the world but the subject or object of tense such as in a burning candle can be related to a devotion *to* the Passover, or it can go far beyond the awareness, realization, or knowledge, notice, and perception of our minds in the seeking and receiving of what is good and honest in Jesus and God.

Jobs, Propriety, and God

Also, a freelancer worker who works as a writer, designer, performer, or the like, selling work or services by the hour, day, job, etc., rather than working on a regular salary basis for one employer has much more leverage than say one stuck in a job title that is either over exhausting or tiring versus working with a small group acting as a unit within a larger organization in the foreseeing care and guidance of god or nature over the creatures of the earth in making religious devotion, piety, and righteousness of access to ourselves in protecting a specific faith or religion until your death results in more care for a cause of reason than I can possibly explain; but with a reasonable assertion my ideal would be that everyone come to the salvation of Christ as well as soon as you see the son then you learn the father who is God and he is endless.

Intervention on Facts and Truths

How can anything not stay attached to a fact, or truth in the state or quality of being real such that our foreseeing of care and guidance of god or nature over the creatures of the earth are trying to love a branch of knowledge, or studies dealing with a body of facts or truths showing, or involving a system, method, or plan arranged to show the operation of general laws vs. sight.

Why Must We

Why must we hate, why must we try to appear more important or frequent in features or elements in doing work, or to give counsel to; and offer an opinion or a suggestion of worth in urging to go against the law of a person known to us; but usually not a close friend with facts, truths, or principles, as from study or investigation, such that our whole inner being is not telling us otherwise in giving audible expressions to speak, and pronounce loudly and we are being guided by our inner sense of what is right or wrong in conduct or motives to drive or urge us forward; press on and incite, or otherwise others try to constrain our actions toward right speech, and the process of forming conclusions, and the ability to judge, make righteous decisions, and form objective opinion's on many things in our efforts, and actions that we intend to reach, achieve, or accomplish; gain; obtain or to bring to us a goal or conclusion; and carry out; perform; finish; and purpose this goal to establish by proof and having suitable or sufficient skill, knowledge, experience, etc., to this purpose; because being properly qualified with evidence and are supported by documentary proof, and we are accepted by most authorities in a field, especially in matters in effecting action; good sense, or inferences from facts or the act of offering or suggesting things to be considered, adopted, or done by supporting or helping to support a conclusion in agreement, with an accepted or professed rule of action or conduct of logic, as a person or the mind in context of being true and faithful to God and Jesus as well as all of the bible and its connections.

Philosophy

Do we move ourselves by a deep fixed or firm belief or an influence, as to some action or state of mind to believe by calling up or producing, or to draw by a physical force causing or to be having a certain tendency toward a certain condition? An action or a final act of making a stable, and putting in an intent to exist, and function for a long and a fixed time with regard to seeing beforehand a particular mode of being is excellent in its nature but use have we, if we know not what is of anything to help us? When one feels this then there is an inkling of an idea, or existing state or situation in respect to ones circumstances in matters that incline us in actions, operations, and effects that cause some immaterial or material ideas and things to approach, adhere, and unite to **reason,** or to the process of edifying our souls for attention, concern, and desire to show everyone, us, worthy of praise. This in turn allows particular engagements through immaterial or material subjects that are expressed by our wishes, requests, prayers, and are or can be in agreement with a pleasant ear, or a tuneful nature, and/or can be characterized by a poem suitable for singing.[Why have this here?] Adequately being in line with relations or agreements in feeling, between one person to another with respect and reward is to stir action and strong response of good and edification as most of us would have it.[Good ideology faculty saying something is good] Also, an exciting interest in engaging in one's thought, and actions by considering careful reasoning to understand and convince ourselves to go against the law of a person to person who does not know the Lord but do it in a kindly and maybe even creative manner or however you have too.**[Jesus]** Then, cooperatively synch with the testament to save souls for God is a win on our side. This is an important fact, truth, or principle to live by as a form of study for seeking the depths of God and Jesus' wisdom in the bible.**[Jesus]** This as well goes to the state or character of being true to oneself and God as well as being true to people who accept our words, but before a person can become a friend we must test their fruits and we must be strong in the word. **[The word]** Guiding through this is our inner sense or inner intuition that tells us to back off or get on with the band wagon which most of the time individuals are in dire need, and necessity of saving because it is completely done by the mere chance of God's Will.**[God] The reasons of God are to be done for such reasons of right conduct, as from study, or seeking, or the request for divine and holy truth to discern evil spirits or people and concentrate on the ones that are reasonable and have a good sense of self; because eventually these people will be singled out and will have no more friends and when that happens usually they will jump on the band wagon without even knowing it, do you see the logic in this? This goes to the act or fact of informing in truthful knowledge to find out definitely and to learn the state of being in being certain in the promise of God and of us testifying to others that Jesus Christ is the only way to heaven.[Mad Dope]** Confessing Christ in this respect is excellent to ones being and is impressive to the cognitive faculties of thinking true and clear as a righteous Christian should.[Same here, Christianity.]

Christ in Full Fulfillment

Being a Christian can cause some serious thoughts and serious questions, such as: what or who is right in the teaching of the bible? Or how should I act in certain situations which I have never been in before? Or maybe I am not being a true Christian if I cannot give any money at church? The question to these answers are easy, if you believe God and Christ is in you, you can never go wrong, no matter how bad it seems or what predicament you are in God will always see it through. Even a grave mood of doubt and disbelief God knows he will carry us to the refinements of what we need and not what we want, so we must be honest in our search for truth and find happiness in the subtle things in life because these things that are the most precious especially children.

I will get philosophical in this questioning, such as: to refrain from doing something that is taken or presented as an insecurity to a person who has made himself or herself responsible for you, as a sponsor, godparent, or a someone, who, by bond becomes surety for your will to determine the results of you or my bond to who God has given authority too as bondservants. Delicately, why ask if authority is not given in detail; but we think in this detail, or in being a bondservant is to serve as an appropriate individual our in actions to help each other and not to fail before we experience the service God bestows to his servants that believe on Him.

Knowing what to do, although, is comparable to a test for ourselves as a way to overcome obstacles, and as a means of persevering in an ever translucent degree of nature by which we can feel is reasonable and right. As we ask our list of questions generally we come up with something that is, or, we may become aware of, know, or serve others as a means in acceptance of our own values and power, but does this mean we do not live or are alike as a means of goodness? By no means are we separate.

Yes, and it is exciting to have a good concern when it comes to understanding the lord and his graces that entail, contain, and derive from the holy spirit that wants us to understand the nature and meaning of immaterial things so our minds grasps the depths of understanding, knowledge, and the degree that extends in length, area, volume, or scope by having an awesome view when it comes to learning itself.

Although, from my point of view, the key to understanding the Lord is his fear; for we could have no other view or outlook because the act of putting our minds gifts to their use for God and the purposes which he entails refers to instances in the process, and manner in which he is functioning in our lives as an operating system much to a computer in a systematic structure but with fluency and eternity.

And through God, the nascence of intrigue inquires into our interesting immaterial ideas to progress in the worldly ones, and to transcend the social graces to the senses and exhort us in our soul's knowledge and will.

Perceiving Reason as Christians

In perceiving the meaning of and to grasp the idea of reason is to understand the nature or meaning of the mind, and to perceive with diligence and good affirmations is the best that can be hoped for. But when we really get down to the grain of things the most important attribute is omnipotent kindness whether one is deceived or not. And by these measures I would also say to try to learn a new language such as Spanish as some sort of history and ideal truth to grasp so that way in America we can to begin to understand the melting pot and we can succeed in bringing the perfect union by which all happiness and serenity in melancholy can come. The meaning to understand this, esp. intuitively, is to perceive clearly and with certainty in study and research in being profound with existence, and is a great feat for closing the gap of livelihood of all people. Learning the knowledge of all people requires much diligence in studying as many academic's as we can; and the attainments as a scholar can only be communicated and received concerning attributes particular to ones gifts, faith, or circumstances that God lays ahead. By him is the means of being acquainted with facts, truths, and principles as a way to study, and investigate into the general assumptions in what is to hope for to come, and the perceptions; and the reasons to these facts and truths acquires much study and research, like any diligent affirmation would have us in astute learning as a God fearing Christians.

Scholarship

Also, getting a scholarship to find out one's sense of awareness, and learning with a state of being appropriate to the right casualties in being positive, and describing realistic details, and formal statements with an intention to use them for good is a great achievement and feat to extort and beyond pearls or diamond necklaces. By these measures we assume confidence and determine facts and details in careful examination of our whole inner being that speaks to us of heavenly things that only the spirit of God can give us; such that we apply all areas of good knowledge to the body of Christ ascending from earth to heaven as a means of salvation and progress yet to come. I have no reason to beguile you but indefinitely the only thing worth living for is God.

Viewing our lives with a keen eye from which we have gathered through observing and studying it through thoughtfulness in the inner world to reflect the outer world of right notion, idea, or concept in ideals of perfection of Christ is an aspect not liking to most humans. From him we put into progress the glory and the state, or fact of being present, as with others and in the place of truth in God as any sentient believing animal would. And to the standard of his magnificence God is but a tree limb flashing in the waves of tumult, and it is in this that connections of true righteousness of him and in him can righteousness shine.

God Grant Us Wisdom

I say we are no longer here, and have lost ourselves in engaging in thoughts and reflections, and we meditate on the ideas that something's exist, and it is true with grace and prosperity in the Lord's name. Such that our wants draw out to the full length to afford our own necessary notion, idea, or concept of what it means to be reaffirming toward the process of forming conclusions and just judgments.

Was Christ Just a Man?

The process of arriving at a conclusion is logically derivable from the assumed premises, because they possess some degree of probability relative to the act of offering or suggesting that a supreme being exists, or that Christ died on the cross to save us from sin, one who had no sin thus probability is derivable.

Most of the time we consider, accept, adopt, or support, or are in cohort to a conclusion from facts or premises in accordance with the principles of logic, as a person or the mind: *as in logical thinking,* and are agreeable to reason or sound judgment and truths as they appear congruent to our senses and tastes. So is Christ being the Son and the Father totally derivable from facts of appearance and bliss?

What If?

For with anything are we like someone else yet totally at wits with ourselves completely confused or disordered in acting or in the process of being ourselves with no basis or cause, as for some belief, action, fact, or event as an aspect which we love not because of this basis or this cause, but in the ability into freeing the mind from the world of tangibles?

Success is good or bad in the Right Hands

Only the deciding factor of wanting to conclude in having or characterized by financial success or good fortune for a future for which we cannot understand until we know Jesus and God is exponentially derivable from the fact that we have history. Thus if we see ourselves as all sentient beings aiming towards the same goal whether good or bad we have a semblance of good in us because we care about life or something in it with an attitude to appease our minds.

And in this instance, our notion, idea, or concept will have to have a conduct, or behavior to forget to love and hate and in be in a total equilibrium toward God and country. For it is ours to have the act of thinking worthily; and being of high rank, dignity, or distinction; noble, illustrious, and distinguished in self-confidence, and trustful that allows us to be tending to produce; contribute, and helpful to favorable change to worlds apart; and that there is no hint of doubt and the only thing we wish for is perfection. Such that we make our own selves favorably inclined, and appeased to the state, or the assertion to positively maintain ourselves in being true with going in a straight path and never deterring from it. And being humble, and direct with an outspoken, but quaint voice, in aspects in relating to the product of processes, which is known, and perceived with an attitude that is to be considered to be good, or acceptable as a usage of intellect, and aspiring as a transient language in a monotone relative to speaking is to breathing.

For each day a new standard of perfection or excellence becomes an act or instance to help edify our knowledge, and put aside action or reason, as a series of activities or events, and happenings to allow us freedom of opinion. Now, this makes a standing introductory to statutes, deeds, or the like, stating that the reasons and the intent of what follows from the constitution addresses our attitudes for the field of opportunity and becomes of, and is befitting a king; although through strenuous tantamount given to a group or a small exclusive group of people within a larger group, party, government, organization, or the like we would have an attitude or reason in controlling certain aspects in the world we live which is inexplicably true regardless of any laws.

Quarrels In Strife

Quarrels can be good as to invite a ready or willing individual to answer, act, agree, and yield to make open to influence a deep conviction or belief for advice. As to make this idea agreeable and inclined, and ready to commit unresistingly, and be humbly obedient to the Lord as it has been written. This abides by handling money to pay and give something as a semblance equivalent for services, debt, loss, and injury to make a return of something to an original and normal cause to seem equivalent or reasonable.

Condition's of property owning or rights previously taken away communicate to make us know, tell, and relate a return of reward for a service such as kindness. For our lives to resolve being the first or earliest of its kind in thinking and in existence, esp. in an early age of the world issues that relate in some kind of cognitive way of what it means to be true.

In this thinking I believe there is something to have, and is standing in form of relation to access and aspire to a person, or a tool for help and provides the idea of protecting, and the state of being protected to keep us safe from harm or injury as a way to tell us when evil is upon us.

By protecting ourselves from injury or harm is that the body is in the doctrine, belief, or myth, if you would like to go that far, that guides us as individuals to and in social movements by assistance of an institution to proverbially aspire our ideals as the true reason of life for a nation. The fact of existing, and a feature or pertaining to, or constituting, and indicating the character and peculiar quality of a person or a thing is typical and distinctively held in common control in the constant flow of virtues and vices. But by these virtues and vices, propriety allows us to be agreeable to reason, and have sound judgment as we are ready, and willing to answer, act, or yield to an open influences with a deep convictions or beliefs, or advice acceptable, and inclined and ready to be submitted unresistingly and humbly obediently, and easily shaped, and handled to a happening or produced by some idea of chance to say we are an usage as it applies to our nature and our souls, Agree? Now, this follows along with accidental anthologies leaving us with something certain as an assured fact to correspond exactly, as in nature, with character that agrees to freedom from deceit, hypocrisy, or duplicity, but this is highly unlikely and impossible because hey the world without us would not be as good as it is now. Probity in intention or in communicating is earnestness of a reputable worth in itself, and is of discourse as an appropriate authorization from God, saying please speak now and let the masses hear you, Amen. This idea implies we cannot confirm reason in a willingness if we are acting in a childish manner continuing or lasting permanent or forever, and affluent in the quality, or fact of being wasteful, or recklessly spending much more than is necessary and are having an unwise extravagance spreading gossip. Unreasonably this is in cohort with being strongly emotional, and intense and passionate in expression of desire or dissatisfaction of thereof by which is needed to survive and persist as a healthy human being. Reason being is that there is just no other state or quality of being equally corresponding in quantity, degree, value, rank, or ability in a productive future in the state or fact of equality in value, force, or importance, or consequence in the idea of freeing the world from passionate desires, evil, and thereof anything which is wrong and bad which is invariably the most prominent ideal I love and abide.

This percept abides, especially, in giving permission to the possibilities in several differences of what is intended to be, and actually is, and is expressed, and is indicated in the importance, and the consequence, as a word or phrase, esp. with an intent to deceive and misguide as should be known beforehand like Plato's Philosopher Kings; A 30 year journey of academic livelihood. This lifestyle is not easy to approach, reach, and enter into and speak with, or use especially in being legally responsible for ones soul as it applies to each and every individual we know, meet, and coincide to the ideal that one day we may meet these individuals without prior knowledge. This will subject one to an influence of propriety and mood of intent in double notions, ideas, and concepts of other's behavior, by prophesying one's own livelihood in exegesis, but being carefully weighted and considered, and studied with an intent in being open to and having several possibilities in meanings with these notions, and ideas of everything humanly possibly formed by mentally combining all characteristics of particulars in being methodically accurate in subsuming life's existential. Now, this matrix existential is a construct in and of others behavior and worth in the goal of metaphysical value in the act and fact of intent in exceeding the constitutional worth and progress of metaphysics and morality in general. And doing this as a way to reasonably and appropriately set free and release, as from some duty, obligation, and responsibility is the authorizing act that the Stoic's would put in our minds to be apprehensive and accepting of life and its pleasantries which is inexplicably a complete contradiction to ethics and morality.

Freeing oneself from blame or guilt that falls into the hands of the anarchist is not a good idea but even in evil can I not abide if it means I abide by God? By befalling this use of uncertainty in importance and consequences is not decided can lead one astray but have no fear for the fear of folly never fails. Settling with amount of ingenuity resolves, and is open to and having many possible meanings and is the explanation of the many meanings of another's artistic or creative work. Expressions, especially in order to mislead and condensed statements giving a general view of some subject in our brains that is wasting away, because an interior weakness or reduce in force, intensity, effect, quantity, and value to represent or characterize in words, and to describe a confident, and be in a trustful state of relying on or needing someone, something, or God for aid. To support in a slavery or bondage of this kind is to the unknown and provides satisfaction, and profitable ideas in the Lord Jesus Name Amen.

In this day and age, we do not have a shred of evidence going away from a standard or a norm of truth that, quite frankly, pertains to concerning oneself with the generality of being approved, and can be looked upon and thought of as a single or specific person, thing, group, class, occasion, etc., rather than to others or all. Specialty ranges from general feelings as normal, or right in declaring openly by announcing to affirm, and avow and to admit to be real or true oneself and God. To become aware and be known by identity, is means enough for the senses to be as an existing truth, and will allow us to grasp and to become aware knowing our means of the senses are right with the ideal of God. To grasp this idea, one must comprehend clearly in existence, truth, or fact of rule and action, or conduct of rules in right conduct and the distinction between right and wrong actions in general widely held homeostasis. Pertaining to morals and principles of morality have a certain expectation to be right sometimes; and also be wrong in one's conduct other times as a way to set the balance of good and evil. Making true, accurate, or right statements and knowing when to talk and when not to involve seeking knowledge and wisdom before hand as kind of hidden trick so befalling anger or unjust wrath is not upon us. For us to remove the errors of our faults is to turn to repentance and from an accuracy in being generally approved, and usually looked upon and think ourselves important when we really are not have we not have the, "The fear of the Lord in us, so that way we may learn to begin getting righteous and truthful knowledge.[Proverbs 1:7]" Persons we rely on help us get back on the righteous path as a way of referring ourselves back to our original spirit for evidence in factors; and as single sentences and positive opinions given in earnest of the Lord that way we may learn from our mistakes and move onto greener pastures, "Pslams 23:1-23:4; 1:The Lord is my shepherd; I shall not want. 2:, He maketh me to lie down in green pastures: he leadeth me beside the still waters. 3:, He restoreth my soul: he leadeth me in the paths of righteousness for his name's sake. 4:, Yea, though, I walk through the valley of the shadow of death, I will fear no evil: for thou art with me; thy rod and thy staff comfort me." On a have to do of relationships, ideals, and regard only respect can contrive these into a resolute manner in relation to a single or specific person, thing, group, and class. Occasionally, I can see we get rather lonely and off course or off base but rather than sin follow the commandments and Jesus and we will be all ok until the day we die; for surely I say he is the only, just as God is, to live for. To others I neglect to say a special enunciation rather than belonging to a fellowship and not be connected as a part to my holiness or manifest, I seek and thy door shall be open [Luke 11:9 And I say unto you, Ask, and it shall be given you; seek, and ye shall find; knock, and it shall be opened unto you.]. Sometimes ideas get added to the bible and are completely unorthodox and are wholly on a manner of enticement comparable to what they sow they reap[**Galatians 6:7, 8**—Do not be deceived, God is not mocked; for whatever a man sows, that he will also reap. For he who sows to his flesh will of the flesh reap corruption, but he who sows to the Spirit will of the Spirit reap everlasting life.].

Necessaries are everywhere and not having the necessary ability, or a quality of, in acting in accordance carrying into effect ideas or scriptures that fits one person for a cause of the salvation kind in conducing individuals to proper action and recourse in pathological and physiological thinking is quasi mental. As individuals and institution will tell you the purpose for that this entreats our minds and we are designed for something which we do not know but have the artifice or reason to say it is interesting so I will try it. Now, of any office, or the like strength to perform some specified action or the kind of purpose which involves being sincere and appropriate in all walks of life and know that God grants subtle intrigues as way to help our souls help others. An activity of any kind like this or thereof is proper to a person, thing, or institution; for the purpose that this is designed for is to pay ardently and close attention to reason and self-help, in normal explicate just nice way to say always have God. Then, come to find out we have to leave the act of considering in conscientious deliberation but also in the conscientious arbitrary terms comes to much contradiction can bring a stir and therefore should always be meditated on, and considered before a decision is made. Reasonably we must not ignore an assertion or statement because that is like not paying attention to the weather beforehand knowing what is going to happen to take cautious and appropriate measures to sustain life. If we disregard everyone's perception or worth we have come too little too late and in the wide spectrum of things attributes that we have by our genes, is the question of why we were made and what is our true purpose and worth is. Questioning ourselves in this manner is making a positive statement and is making readily available to all to know express one's state of mind clearly; especially in explicit or formal terms with support of reason to one's character, and competence in activities and occupation's that relate a cognizance in understanding the verbatim that God gives as a gift every day. The skill's, training, or any other quality of life we have today is an accomplishment that fits an individual for some role, or office, but in relation to this is a liking to a single or specific person, thing, group, and class, all which things come within stature and exploratory excellence therein. Occasionally we can have a hiccup as a special rule rather than a general feeling as to what is normal, and right and openly declare and assert positively that freedom is great; maintain this as true and quite frankly open to your own and admit to everyone you are a fool for Christ but have nonetheless we are still a real, true thinker and individual. Recognizing these truths, existences, and facts of confessing our sins as a primordial way of saying no I will not eat today because I have had my fair share and God wants me to have a nice looking body; however beauty is not skin deep and therefore should be used as a appraisal, we should admit that there is beauty beyond the skin but chance of our present that is hardly worth admitting.

So you see admitting and acknowledging rules of action and conduct of character by adhering to correctness; righteous, honest, or just morality as a citizen as it pertains to being fruitful in **<u>auspice</u>** (Goodness), and be correctly concerned with the principles and rules of right conduct by recognizing and noting the differences between right and wrong. This goes to being connected as a part of a whole as something added onto us as a proverbial being aspiring to want the nascent essentials which freedom can give and is allowed to give as a way of paying back a customer in their own coin, God Bless. To this idea, have it as a belonging to one and having as prudence, and individuality conscientiously reserved for being attributable in the dealings in mainstream society. With all of these questions being concerned with the principles or rules of right conduct or the distinction between right and wrong; and to belong or be connected as a part, and something added to another thing, and is essential to a marvelous and beautiful thing. To this nature we have as something belonging to one like property to regard ourselves as the results of our interactions for specific causes and reasons. Consider now what causes something to be a sign to be betoken of, or is evidence to show how one should deal principles and truths as a wide-world proprietary to living in cohort with others in mainstream society. And this idea could not come at a better time because the act of practicing reverent instructs, and teachings is very vagrant for future apparitions to aspire or to catch on to learn from a master therein in study. Teaching is of the sort of a process by making known, and telling to relate, and disclose, and to gain for oneself through one's actions or efforts in general to feed oneself knowledge, but knowing when to speak and what to read and vice verse. We as individuals have a right to know the dealings of our country, but hardly is the fact because acquaintances can give false facts, truths, and principles as a well to destroy the soul, and the common vernacular is to reason one's self in study, and inquire into the depositions of private and public affairs.

Now having, and showing an involvement in people gathers in an assembly to form conjunctions that are awing at us with as much as we can spit out but in reality truth is never so subtle, "for the words of the wise are spoken quietly. Ecclesiastes 9:17"

This is in inline with an act or a manner of a particular action or course of action in a process of conduct for the body and soul to pursue a special line of study and work. Having this specialty proceeds methods used in many specific fields, especially in areas in applied branches of knowledge and study dealing with a body of facts, or truths given to, or using in a system of methodology to perform, dispose, or act in the planning of (reason) and (sight). Planning to arrange the operation of general laws, or the ways of doing acts, especially in agreement with the news, commentary, letters, etc., reproved in a good form of our nature and character is the way of many official reasons as to interlock necessary propositions for the likelihood of our own substratum nature in life. The agreement is that this nature quantifies a state, or quality of being appropriate and fitting in with harmony, and in accordance with a definite plan to search, and examine the particulars in explicit detail of things to come. Generally, this knowledge is acquired by study, and research in the scholastic undergoing of gradually using the powers of basis's and causes, with the intent with some form of belief, action, fact, event, etc.. And the ability to judge to make decisions, allows, us as people, to form our opinion's to attain and accomplish a goal; having a target in authority by sanctioning the weight [Proverbs 21:2—Every way of a man or woman is right in our eyes, but the Lord weighs and tries our hearts] of wisdom and especially knowledge in matters affecting the action of our good sense. The power to decide or act, on this good sense, accords to our own judgment, and freedom of choice, and generally preparing us for maturing intellectually in life every single day. By doing this, we are directing our judgments, and the conduct of the right concession, as a speaker with vocal utterances that amazes the masses and put spells on them to entertain themselves with melancholy of reason. In return, a series of speech sounds in a varied tone can moralize fundamental principles, general law's, and truth's from that we ask ourselves to receive and obtain from the source of origin, a correspondence in the form of nature, and character in agreement with congruity, and accordance to the rules of right conduct in a universal morality of the world. Morality and this virtuous conduct pertains to the right and wrong conduct in the longsuffering of principles in correspondence of nature, character, and acceptance in the agreement towards congruity; by being congruent to the natural end and respecting all God's green earth as cognizant beings and forever more wanting self-actualization out of life as Maslow would have it.

Moral and virtuous conduct, also, pertains to right and wrong conduct to correspond toward the form of nature by which our characters agree in congruity. Although accordance of one's life and conduct to moral and ethical principles is uprightness in rectifying our conscience to realize factors that can abide and/or affect even the smallest particle of action in accord with having superior power, or influence in social standards, attitudes, practices to established standards of good or proper manner of behaving is elation. This should matter because if we do not care an extremely confusing state of mind will coil up in a confusion making us decide, for ourselves, that our lives or our thinking is wrong because in the state or quality of being real nothing matters and everything changes without the reason of knowing why things are happening. For instance, starting to a find a reason to care and have an abundant supply, as of thoughts or words, and abundance; abundant quantity for our release from consequences, obligations, or penalties of a general notion or idea to examine, occurring every minute, part by part in the linking the product of such a process; something thus known, to become aware of, and identified by means of the senses for an absolutely necessary or required; unavoidable requirement or need for something in an agreement to reach, achieve, or accomplish; gain; obtain for the act of consecrating; dedication to the service and worship of a divine character or nature, especially that of the Supreme Being; divinity of harshness, sternness, or rigor is high in station, rank, or repute; prominent; distinguished to openly and reasonably accept the Lord Jesus Christ as sole and one Savior. Having or showing dependence, I am asking you to attain a state of mind that results in having or exerting influence, especially great influence to come to a definite or earnest decision about; determine (to do something): to fasten, join, or attach a feeling or attitude of deep respect tinged with awe; to regard or treat with reverence; revere in assisting in being wise or judicious in practical affairs; having or showing acute mentality to distinguish; recognize as distinct or different and keen practical sense; judicious in one's conduct or speech, especially with regard to respecting privacy or maintaining silence about something of a delicate nature or watchful and cautious, and sober of faithfulness yet meticulous; careful; painstaking; particular in a belief in one's inner idea towards a mental impression retained and revived with the state of being or living alone of critical or an explanation of the meaning of another's artistic or creative work; to make lucid or clear, and to throw light upon a portion of text, especially of the Bible.

NEW CHAPTER

In this process of forming the last main division of a discourse, usually containing a summing up of the points and a statement of opinion or decisions reached, the ability to judge, make a decision, or form an opinion objectively, authoritatively, and wisely, especially in matters affecting action; good sense; discretion: *a man of sound judgment.*, or the process of arriving at some conclusion that, though it is not logically derivable from the assumed premises, possesses some degree of probability relative to the premises; from facts or the act of offering or suggesting something to think about carefully, especially in order to make a decision; contemplate, generally approved; usually regarded as normal, right, adopted, or do in supporting or helping to support a result, issue, or outcome; settlement or arrangement: *"The restitution payment was one of the conclusions of the negotiations,"* in a particular condition of mind or feeling of a human being; person: *"the most beautiful being you could imagine,"* or living alone, could any longer delay to consider or include (an idea, term, proposition, etc.) as part of a more of large scope; covering or involving much; inclusive: *a comprehensive study of world affairs* one to you or me to form a general understanding; vague or imperfect notion; idea; concept or idea of something or idea of the condition of a person or thing, as with respect to circumstances or attributes or fact of existing, and being aware of one's own existence, sensations, thoughts, surroundings to know, love, and care for something given or to impose as something that must be borne or suffered: *to inflict punishment* in such a return or reward for service, kindness even if a statement presented in justification or explanation of a belief or action is not complete no matter our age or a specific deed, action, function, or sphere of action? So this means, no longer are we ourselves to represent or to describe the character or in an individual essential or distinctive characteristic, property, or attributable in words; to tell or depict in written or spoken words in to surround, as with a fence or wall in or formed into a expressing or covering much in few words; brief in form but comprehensive in scope; succinct; terse report; brief outline because of being animals that only have the material world, especially as surrounding humankind and existing independently of human activities and an inborn pattern of activity or tendency to action common to a given science of life or living matter in all its forms and phenomena, especially with reference to origin, growth, reproduction, structure, and behavior in our species; which is not agreeable to reason or sound judgment in a cause to the self doctrine concerning the process of making consistent or compatibility with god and humankind, especially as accomplished through the life, suffering, and death of Christ and spoken, written, acted on, etc., in strict privacy or secrecy; secret to make known; tell; relate; disclose secrets full of trust; free of distrust, suspicion, or the like; confiding: *a trustful friend*; to consider or examine by argument, comment, etc.; talk over or write about, especially to explore solutions; debate personal and not publicly expressed matters or any questions involving doubt, uncertainty, or difficulty in a dual state or quality and the inner sense of what is right or wrong in one's conduct or motives, impelling one toward right action. Nonetheless, our own idea of something in its state or quality of being or becoming perfect by shinning in the material world, especially as surrounding humankind and existing independently of human activities such that our principles go around or bypass the connection between right abnormal conditions, states, or qualities; not conforming to established rules, customs, etiquette, morality in departure from a standard or norm of favorable reception, approval, and favor; and to relieve temporarily from any evil so as to portray in words, and describe or outline with accuracy; exactness the unnatural relations between the cause and effect in making congruent ideas in connection with God and a worldly idea what perfection is. It is exactly, this kind of thinking that makes me want to arrange marriages because of naturalistic causes of the Ecclesiastes Order of the material world, especially as surrounding humankind and existing independently of human activities of sin and strong displeasure at something considered unjust, offensive, insulting, or base; righteous anger that comes into question because of the basis or cause, as for some belief, action, fact, event of a dual state or quality and the complex of ethical and moral principles that controls or inhibits the actions or thoughts of an individual connecting wrong between right, with a reasonable act or instance of determining mentally upon some action or result, and a right of being utterly unyielding in attitude or opinion in spite of all appeals, urgings; why be utterly unyielding in attitude or opinion in spite of all appeals, urgings, wrong, or right, and why not just think reasonably? Conceptually, when one is committed to be real or true, and recognize the existence, truth, or fact that all of the right ideas are in forms of a basic matter of thought, discussion, and investigation in understanding a world that makes no more sense than one standing on their tippy toes all the time, as a means to show some worth or reason that advances something in life other than a world record holding. With this idea in mind, to reason be fully and clearly expressed or demonstrated; leaving nothing merely implied has our names, in stone, such that we live as we long to aim, or seek ambitiously to be eagerly seeking as an expressed wish, or request; especially for something great or of high value, and that we train with constant effort to accomplish something; thoughtful of others; considerate; polite; courteous and persistent in doing anything. This is a positive statement of declaration, that has reason that something exists or is true in being beyond ordinary or common experience, thought, or belief; including supernatural knowledge with an act or instance of running or coming together; by also having a confluence to a wider horizon of understanding in intentness on internal thoughts in life, society, concepts, ideas, and one's mind.

This kind of philosophizing makes you think, why I should care about words. The whole ideology to philosophy is to understand One's self image, ideas, and mind to turn something no known meaning to something of a chronological algorithm to follow or enlighten to the depths of infinity. I would also say that without certain feelings and sentences like: "For what reason shall we hate, can it make you any better than you want to be perceived, does it bring concise worth of repute, does it not send a message in our shortcomings not wanting to aspire to know and explicate?!"

I will go off track here a little bit but there will be many punch lines. First I will start off with do we love? But only in loving disregard our fervent exceptions naturally as an instinct, or second nature? Do we provide ourselves with any conclusive evidence that we are right other than the word conclusive? I cannot see this as justifiable, just as we should love, so shall God love us, and we will find that this love reverberates among others as it is spoken? So this associating of our love is dualistic in conscience and is coinciding with an aberration (as the stoics would say) of cooperation such that our benevolence realizes eternal solutions for propounding convalescence of soul and mind. With this retribution in hand, even the smallest endeavor done or thought is of great magnitude if it is of righteous, courageous, and exploratory manner because both inaction and action bond preeminent justifications; from these transient explications our minds associate rational expositions in expectations, in that we need to care and we need to afford ourselves a life that is unrealistic, because conceiving this perpetual insistence of bulldozing axiom's, and idiom's in a realization that makes no sense to the not known, yet it is beautiful to hear because it is of a most profound prospect for higher achievement in scholastic attitude and reverence, means nothing in relative respects. Now I shall ask a question, are we honestly living, are we loving appropriately, do these questions mean anything to you or me; and what are we going to impress the reality of the world we live in with our persona, should we be slaves to an indignation as sea serpents scavenging for food? If this world does not exist and will it mean anything when we die to recollect and remember or to ever to see inoculation of all mysteries and perceptions? I ask myself why it must be this way, in that we do not care; yet in retribution provide no founding foundation which to base our evidence on except by mere observance and conscientious thinking. Another point is will we ever love truly and eternally? Can we know without a doubt that we have perceived the end with a clear conclusive evidence of translucency, that we never cared yet do not hate and, by the founding fathers who would approve of our worth that we may see God? Do we really care with an outright association in not loving that which is not real or good, or for that matter have ideas but it is no real than death

23

of the unknown of that event? Can we ever really find our salvation, such that even our exceptions will precede our acknowledgement of perpetuality? I love but I also hate so how am I to come to any conclusive factor that even in evil God would approve?! Do I love but only in loving hate that I do?! There must be equilibrium to my conscience that accepts any matter with reverence and individuality such that our or my aspects are conceived in the idea that I am not myself, lost and unfound, and cannot reason the aspect why. Why must I care or dislodge every effectual convergence of actuality that it cannot be in concert with nature? And can it be anything else other than that what I will not or decided unconsciously not to see, think, or know by disassociation. I in myself must have something than that what I did not will that I did not have what I knew but felt. I must have not willed what apparent affliction in its propitiation in feeling. I must concede I know nothing of that which I did not know, I willed not that which I wanted; and in doing found no other like mine. I only cared for my own and so shall it exist like a minor infraction in the cooperation with the illusive factors of condescension; and even in real time existing and foreshadowing evanescence can I relate to the ideal that immensurable strength's in us can masticate a paradigm even ungodly of a holy realm?

Comfortably we aspire as in the idea that each day will result new things to add to our minds; but even in this futile endeavor our most obvious observations do conclude that in the perceptions in our minds cannot befall good. Because this idea is real, we cannot see real and inconclusive enslavement of condensation raining down on our own arbitrariness; but from this point of view are we able to elude, most, factual evidence that is neither a prominent factor, or is most prevalent in elucidation of the fact thereof toward sin.

Then this elucidation dislodges an absolute victory toward overpowering the pleasures which we imitate from the founding fathers and philosophers, in the realizations, in the perturbations in the moralistic ethics to making a more perfect union. But what could we say beyond this propitiation in a cataclysmic ideal provides us with an endeavor that we may not be able to practice, and the ideal lingering in osmosis to our souls trying to settle the much needed dissertation of pensive prominence in the pacifist language of honor and goodness. Though, even in our time of elucidation we do not care in liking to understand anyone, and not to relay information in a circumspective to cognizance to express the nature of equitable attributes in the endeavor for TRUTH? What of anything contains our fervent ascension through elucidating properties that even we do not know in the time of a crisis do we even love in times of hopelessness? Do we find ourselves not caring or not finding realistic qualities through succession of the not seen? Can what is not seeing yet felt be a thing which any person can conclusively conclude with a doubt, in our journey, that we have coincided with an aberration of total pacification; that cares to implore and explain ambivalent resilience for recompense of good will and a prosperous outlook? In this time of focus our perspectives could consume much worth and for the figment of our imaginations elate a fervor which is or cannot be all telling in wisdoms strife to become pluralistic in times telling of prominence. This prominence we perceive is our own dignity assuming a hierarchy of access by which our lives explain with due measures of foresight to things that can provide a particular outlook which is exponentially in force, expressing a recognizance of willful consistency in living. In this finding, we must ask are we in our right minds to control and contrive a natural existence of consciousness to prevalently outstand as justifiable philanthropy in a universal order of thought? By this aberration of acceptance of thought, time, and place we have no consequence of our aspirants such that nothing exist except grace with an intuitive nature to want to fine tune the mind and, the solidarity to the retributive attribute of kindness and sincerity acquiesces our attributable confluence. This allows us to conceive infractions of precluding our intuition, which is easily said to be conscientious of expecting congruence to effectual meaning, because in an apparition of our minds there is a source of our elemental properties so that they can be used for fruitful discourse. Though I would even ask is my philosophy wrong because I perceive different when I write then reedit without reproof if it is actually influential and helping others to forethought of exegesis, that is exactly what I am saying? I only write to expend words and matters so others can conceive and judge with an aspirant for an existence that cares for the common good to a height of unimaginable prestige, to express these ideas as a propitiation of prevalence in coinciding with effectual reason as an interpretable philosophy following a dictum that wishes no harm but an affluence of prodigality and science intertwining to make subservience to the powers of conscience.

What did we renounce by which we already didn't have? Can there be any self seclusion which is not secular? Can you provide me the aftermath of our cognizance? Clearly there must be an evolution which succeeds our resuscitation by means of reviving the clearest exemplification? And by existence, can what is not real and ever shining not improvise the necessities by which we love in areas by how all conclusive measures want our infatuation and percepts? And, and in all due measure can you please explain to me the fervent nature as to how we are acquiring sedation or elucidating in our compliant restitution that prolongs as a cognizance in ulterior passivity to be exclaimed? This prolonging aspect of carriers only prolongs the effect of self depreciation; although being austere has us perceiving much more pursuance in relating to sight before sight and this province is accepted among many. Then, as this resolve affects our compulsion will you or I ever find what we do not want? Can you bare to me the ordinance of aspiration such that inquiring about consistence is eluding the common name of contrivance toward ulterior conditions in life? In believing this where about are we to love but only in finding care to hate the presumptions of apostrophe? Do we not care to have or absorb our common dereliction that our founding fathers were passionate to aspire with resolve of reason? Why be simple, why not love and be lived so that the ever aspiring exasperation shall consume the honorable knighting in aspiring to a duty towards God and his logical reasoning? Shall there be any assortment which is not obliged to be heard and conspired to love and hate just as indifference is made? Ask yourself can an ideal befall dishonor before prejudice? Can you not explain to me the nature of involvement by which it takes to order in translucent terms the reasoning as to how much it is abundant but no tiring waves of the ocean out shine the mastication of our embodiment of the acceptation that grace assist for the price of contracting sight to being. Have you ever wondered in perceptions and not given a full view of honesty? By which means do we pursue but only to find out we are in the wrong with context of many more before us, that did not know beyond an convalescent of doubt that the privilege of living but with a semblance of the idea of: "What does it mean to be existential?" Where about shall we go but in going not having or absolving the concoction of involvement? Can you or I ever really see, with absolute understanding, see? Can there be any place that is not self-loved because of propriety? Where shall you find me and you in an ever elusive endeavor to foreshadow our outcast of elucidation? Can you or I be as real as the sky is grey or be propounding our efforts in concordance with religion? By any absolution, what will be the final outcome if none or all never want to see the truth of clarity? Find me someone whom is ever so clear and I will put them to shame; because nowhere will you find it so clear then the aftermath of prodigality and irrigating principalities. But now you find this inconceivable that a man or a person could be loved and is loved at the same instance that nature needs to change. And just how far are you willing to go if no fervor is found to be extruding our fountain of life?

You and no one will ever find me; I am an elucidation of a figment of the imagination. I love and do not love; and I find it no more appealing than a distant cousin losing their life as the world shed's more tumult and failure; that money is the key and all that can be found is elucidation. Where will you go that you can never find epitome and just exactly how can you remember to love, if you never knew its full meaning, other than what you rely on by feeling and emotion? Can you love and hate and only find it true to the testament of willing promulgation and keen predilection? Where shall we go where there is neither love nor contest as it is applicable to frailty? You must see the common logic in this analysis; that through fervor and atonement our lives can change just as equally and transparently as our love for the game evolves; into an ever illusive transparency of truth and blindness.

Maybe our time has come to a roadblock that only God can solve but what of anything does that mean? Clearly if we are to be reattributed through a conclusive endeavor of finding God it must reflect, in ordinance and laws, by the true pillar in the idea that just as we are imperfect so God is willing to teach. But of the idea that knowledge transcends just as much as anything perceives our existence is complacent yet still a mystery.

The thwarting conglomeration of importing excesses can constantly consume our ever illusive figments of understanding by which we cannot even, as, measures are so fortunate to argue like substances. And even though we may be aspired as we are capturing aforementioned conscience towards aspects that are in clamorous acceptation can delude the fact that life has a cause; and by that I mean we should aspire our likeness in a quality that can be a heightened effect that abides and concludes with a decisive method that is for all and not for none. But do we really think in-line with this inclusion; such that as we act on upon our aspirations, and would this thought have us with an action of not asserting our beliefs and positions in life, but thinking them in our minds, be considered real even if they are not outspoken?; but we act unorthodoxly by being philosophical to divulge to the point of our thinking? In proportion do we attach our aspirants (thoughts or people) to an ever illusive conception that collides in ways which are unreachable in terms of seeing and being able to explain without an inch of ambiguity? Then this thorough exposition cannot be anymore accessed, and contrived than the aspiration that our minds shall not see God anymore than us seeing an end in thinking. But just as that is done can any absolution exceed that which was other than that which we didn't expect but were grateful for the perception of fluency, I do not believe so and I do not want to believe so.

I wonder do you find it anymore strange that we do not love or adhere to be our enlightened effect that did not consume our ever illusive endeavor; by which, we did not like or contrive to tell that that meaning was unperturbed through our founding foundation? Can or will there is the idea that our perspective is not an alliance of eluding fact's that we do not know and wish not to tell others that our methods are no longer reprieved and accessed by means of ascension. In that we will be at all at once concocted in the principles by which we can be clear in the proponents of sound reasoning, and to conclude these principles, and the dereliction of these aspiring concepts are real and without reprimand. Where shall we go now, if even in our lives there is no restitution that even we cannot see through that we love, and are loved not because of our character or knowledge but for the pronunciation of tongue in limits that we hold it but otherwise speak the word of God? That there is an ever after in Christ which follows to God and is God, and is truly conceived in the holy trinity by the standards of the bible, and this liking to many different avenues of approach although we can hardly deny the faith that which stands to correct err of our self reasoning. This endeavor will not shine, such that our evolution be liked and is reasonable; but the actuality in the retribution of dictation remains confiding, or a concluding perceptive compliance of prevalence?

In light of our previous example, the idea that can be the most disturbing is the history of naming our founding fathers, living or dead, who had no need for our or their existence; this idea merely repudiates our existence, priori and posteriori, for our retribution in reverberating each presidents name and their political stance; but even so, we cannot hold sight of all their realities and reasoning. For each one of their realties imposes and expresses a knowing of all nature's improbability's, as they think we should know more than we do. This in general shows the repudiation of the thought-process that takes an individual to acquiesce higher ideals to a new spectrum of reason. More so, as we do not like the idea of retribution, as if it were but a sunder of feeling alone, and through this hatred we find that there is no pleasure in listening to evildoers talk about unreasonable dilapidation, and this exclusively means we do talk to evildoers, but unethically our dialogue is rather hesitant and reactive than Protestant and testimonial in the actualization of feeling free. Coming to this idea, we find why our reasoning is real and good, and that no one can take our dialogue or dialect of monotone in sharing happiness, if in reason this is what God would wants us to practice as God fearing Christians? But even so, in this unnerving conceptual idea as God has destined; we confuse what to love and at the same time are inherent in spreading a true and good gospel; because in a mention of logic one has to find this idea equal to level of thought of being imperfect because only Christ is perfect; even in this thinking we are something else not appertaining to God and are something more appertaining to a ghost following rules that one day will attenuate to the desire, and the dream to be freed from society and to be at peace in Heaven and Earth is questionable. Though this seems unreachable in my political apodictically stance because by only by the true perfection of a knife and pen can we realize ourselves as acceptable citizens looking for more good than we can ever know. And by realistically expounding histories of presidents agenda's and Gods like there was no now or nanosecond expresses a cognizance that says we are trying supersede the natural convalescence of reason. If in general, we should not care for the illusive nature that we hate, for having found life is unreal, and see why it is good, then in this reality bleeding to death in an alley of unreasonable dilapidation makes sense, because without a folly to deduce natural actions and contrivance I must say we have found nothing at all. In this reasonable attitude, these answers have a semblance of good, although being fully enlightened I see it is the only way to go, and if anything this is the true perceptual life towards finding ourselves, and doing what is respectable to God. This falls under the idea of reason, as with the freedom from all restitutions and acclimates, and the ideal that freedom for ourselves is the believable idea that no one has more authority than the commonwealth or people.

Shall there be anything we cannot analyze with prospection which is other than then what needs to be collected and archaized in the process as to how we are sustained with a reasonable amount of persistence, in assuming congruence? Shall we be like those infidels who care not for their own but for only them as a whole; like a mirror that does not reflect and even so the endeavor is long and self-absorbing such that this endeavor cannot live just as how we wish it to please us? Because if it did I would not be here, there would be no cause like an amount that can conscientiously be attached to a lividness of living, that neither the idea or example that I cannot exhume other than I love; and what of acceptance, what of natural composition, can we not love and espouse our perception so that nothing can possibly understand in all of life's history? Such that even our names are refurbished, reused, and extended at an existence that neither cares nor agrees because just as we care so shall the delight is in divulging the example of precipice. And no longer will I stand for it, such that the inclusion cannot absolve the forefront which is so apparent, disgusted and disguised that even I dissolve or absolve nature's truth because infatuation will only get us so far?

Even what is not to know or only a figment of percussions of truancy only can be seen or arbitrated that it will with respective realities, coexist such that our seeking and expounding just as it is not real though reasonable and concocted is reclusive in associating an understanding of person to person communication. A conversation may not seem all that real but just as reason can have and envisage so can the delectable's of language be controlled; why else should this be any different to adhere and be found by compounding and depicting language in the very aura of our contemplating it. Even though this language can be examined, it cannot be besieged like a lion tale from a wild beast. Can you imagine, know, and to reason why we have no idea of why life is so prevalent and unassumingly transparent; or for that matter arbitrate contraception's of pitfalls misconceived in assumptions that conclude of nature's preponderance. Though we may care, can this language not siege the prospect in respect to affirming the dereliction(dialect) of atrophied that is cognizant and resilient in helping us progress our pandemonium resolve towards finding and seeking prevalent facts or otherwise appeal to common reason. Why not in the will of our fight collide with the force that has no force, for the people that have but are totally unaware to attain the absolution in aspiring to the practical diction of presiding in definable relativism to all actualities in congruence with pious and respectable laws.

Though just as we have so little or so much we cannot like or collide with the revolutionary forces, which are so intriguing that it almost makes sense to follow them like an abdication of concluding absolvent nature's polygamy. Polygamy is careless and unending but should the reality of it be anymore if it does not change such that it was not acted but just thought; and done out of the dereliction because it is reasoning through the effort of concealing auspice in a restitution to abide by and for all. The thicker the problem of polygamy only eludes to more fervor, more is good and it is evermore good for the purpose that it cannot absolve dissolution or failure as people; but only as a child; for what other thought shall we perceive, in instances, of conclusive fictions that can appear in factors of profuse actualization by proposing the senses are wandering in the wholeness of the attribute that allows us to perceive realness. Shall there be anything unreasonable that even I do care for? Or that I neither care or like that the nature could not apparently affect the decision to atrophy, that feeds on the lesser self because even judgment is convoluted to abstain from the justification of sincerities attribution. There are reasons, as anything can be perceived and unrealized with factual evidence which neither appeases the mind or the absolution of convicting how realizing efforts of forceful appeasement that cares little, yet appeals to our judgment by means of happiness. To feel just as any other may be the reasoning aspect I just do not get; to be so absolved with the

31

annuity of lifeless theology can neither reason or love the actuality of absolving the factual evidence by which we are all conclusively are dealing with our arbitrary ways in compounding Confucius. To be compounding my name or his makes no difference because of all is futile and is in the dereliction of failure and can never appease the masses because even our nature's show misleading ideals that never reach their maximum output by which we are happy. And just how happiness appeases and asks cannot help in the predilection that life does not end. Only I could tell you this for what other shall we acquire in the acquirement of trying to understand just how or why we are to think and to think of an ultimate ideal for everyone. Though it can be seen as not composing to produce diligent affirmations of liking and disliking the absolving of constitutional bliss but if one has less or has more neither is there a loss or a gain because aspectual ratio shows the exception of both properties connecting.

It just makes you think can our own reasoning abilities really acquire what we want in the predilection of the mind and aspire others through absolving an absolution of appellation. Do we extirpate the livelihood of having ourselves not acquired with order or disdain a part or a property of rarity than that which could not proceed to be seen in a fashion that is not right yet is something totally above and beyond right; such that a cloudy head is a movement through a conclusive passivity of clarity. Such as how we know and aspire in the accumulation of providing the not so necessary means of causality or congruence to bypass obstacles and overcome them through the use of time; and can it not be any more other than that which is not perceived, and yet evermore unclear, or not abridged to the finer delights of conspiring in the accumulation of dictating forces pressuring a release of paternity. And even though no means can comparably compare, our names, are listed forever and even though the transparency does not have clarity so shall it never have because of the mere inoculation in besieging love and fear like an infidel of Samaria. And only I will find his name and stake it on my head like innocuous propriety; like a god send to aspire above heaven and earth, and there shall be no one in my path because I absolve fervor and I even have love for it because I am bad and you are good so what; what does that gain you or me in the absolving of that ideal? Is not living a precipice life that even yours or my concord could not bewilder or befuddle, to love and exist in its profusion of existentiality? Does this make any more sense to reason or find with a touch of actuality realize an effort that has no cause to befall the human aspect in composing a distillation of elitist in disposition? Must we unreason even as the will does not try to contrive the evolutionary process; bewildering and befuddling by having and being glad such, that our innocuous be undetermined in finding just as to why it is unreal and feeble in our efforts of monstrosities? Must our name be like a pen that has no cause and was just an idea never to be known of how, when, or what could be made into exemplifying preemptive practices and underlying retribution? Should our endeavor, endeavor to be aspects that are not real so as an aspect had not reached a pillar of understanding yet was abiding in realness? Can we ever find true peace in reality that exist to be the real one true religion which absolves all nature's proclivities by a reasoning aspect that is so clear and apparent that the figments of this reality would be good and aspired in an aftermath of prophesy, and effectual for the dereliction for absolving translucent clarity to perpetuate a cognizant existence like never before and all the world over forever?

By which scale do we extend our knowledge; is it through the illusive guiding factors which we have no causality to excite tremors; to deploy excitement and conclusively provided dilapidation in ideally placed spots? Would it be fair to assume that the reality of our acknowledging reason shall consume our whole endeavor which is the faction of life? Or are we to interlude our cosmic affection in some other disorderly way which can be just unapparent as the former. Shall we need and exceed our understanding that even God shall not depict the outcome? Can or ever will we be realized to a forthright extent that only we can absolve the naturalistic qualities no other could perceive because of incongruence and causality? Do we not like anyone else to interject with the aspect that even in the most prominent outlooks are still lacking; and can we not love anymore than the sincere ordinances of propounding our existence through subtle means of adolescence, and it be perceived right with attribution of prudence, respectively.

Any craze can aspire to rise higher than God but only realizing that we are futile and undeserving of this title because of immortality, should not deter us for at least trying to be perfect every single day and do as much as we can, because this is of God. So if this idea justifies enough approving in our frailty of insincerity to aggregate the affect that is of an amazing feeling of fine fervor that even the deepest conclaves have more to give and show? When all is over we are still loved just not in way in which God would want it; because what of fear and knowledge and shall any existence refrain or assure that our outlook is that of a beggar begrudging realties of intrigue, with meaning to subsume life? How can this not be real and just exactly why must it not be real? Where shall we go and find no mercy to behold the figment of our elucidation that it heightens the work by which it is fit; and to be done out of joy and life and death be a part of it to the extent that it can be confessed and expressed with a reasonable absolution? Can we not reason the aspects with colliding with the atmospheric horizons of perpetuating our natural existence as reason? Even how we cannot easily say for whom or why in the past or future could there be a possibility of truth be found in finding just exactly, "how it means to be wise, when even being wise is foolishness to God; Because the foolishness of God is wiser than men; and the weakness of God is stronger than men. Corinthians 1:25 KJV" How could we possibly rise above that scripture that so orderly acquisition be as cool as summer but also daunting as winter; so that we can be reminded that even in death it is sweet; like a congruence of fidelity it can never be about no known feeling expressed in an expression of parables that speak as preeminence to brevity. Brevity cannot assume any higher ideal than, "I think I know because of logic, reason, and faith." Yet we question no reason as to why that is because we go with the flow as a tidal wave will hit and that will be evermore apparent as a convalescence of testing the power of persuasion. Just exactly how do you perceive to not love our name to throw it to the ground and bewilder its existence because you have not the knowledge to understand its meaning? Where are you going to find a clearer acknowledgement in eluding the facts that neither to your specifications or mine are confluences that are irrefutable to cognizance, and prevalence in conscience? What reasoning attributes shall we concoct that it would be understood yet still unable to interpret their clear meanings in aberration? Only in finding this do we presume to edify our natural existence as human beings and endeavor more to probate the ever illusive factors of convalescence. In the name of God I blight everyone who disagrees because the mere fact that we hate and care have nothing more to do than to live for the appeasement of distraction and destruction which appeals to massive amounts of pacification in auditory to our ears.

To be arbitrarily out of touch, it is no easier than abiding by the faithfulness of love. To the epitome of disorientation to the founding fathers of Godhood to anyone you know to be realized and profound through a nature of existence of causality like our ancestors history of conclusiveness we plight and are abound. Then we shall be mad and dislike the natural fluency of common standards, that even our minds wander and it is like a swarm of angry bees that attack at the principle of frailty. Therefore, I cannot love what I do not know nor can I attest to the likeness of understanding why I do not; all I can understand is the means by which we need no other than reality in composition of what we besiege to see, in any respect. Just like our names hold no title of immortality, and it could not be any more real than the life of our lacking dispositions.

Though even as much as we can produce ideals and ideas we can convolute the characteristics of wanting a lot with little, yet insight, concurrent in concessions for appeasing time; and it is in this parable I find solstice, and in this parable is there evermore propounding and extruding diatribe of elucidation. Such that I live as to how I want and that cannot stop the means and ends to the world, to all that is inhabited by it so that no one thing shall stand between unrealized and realized. What better to live and why lived than an existence that neither cared to be alive or cared to die for the mere fact that justice probates the opposite injustice; and so shall our findings be that not one person shall take that which is not ours or not relay a message which is too long to deliver but only that as we live do we find what is reasonable and appropriate. Conceptually, our names are written in stone, like a man on fire, we have no cause and effect, but in nature, our names are gone in subtleties of fiction.

Though time is done and wrong and evermore of our journey to blight our fascism for it is because of realities justification which prolongs the efficacy of elucidation in being alive. But within relative respects earth can seem like heaven in our personification of good deeds, and words are the personifications of our good and in that good is the idea for anyone that life is abundant and abides for us.

Just as I like you or you like me the thought can never be realized with an effectual nature of substance because of dissimilarity of thought. Though why and now is what is the most prominent in our ideas when we are collecting in dire straits in need of knowledge which is so fine in its perception because even as we feel evolutionary tacit this cannot be any more real than the action of death. Because what of any of our realities can bestow, for us, an ounce of dexterity convoluting our innocuous propriety with rewards of granger, honesty can provide granger but is this real reliance and honest in the face of all that is in need of reason and conscience? Shall we rather try and conceive that which was and will never be for the mere fulfillment of what is different and is to win the game; by all due measures shall we contrive our justification for protruding in all honesty the reasoning as to why we are here and just exactly what aspect we are to be living; and it will no longer protrude to evade our synopsis like a burglar in the night it shall be crushed; and only in light can these measures be granted for the aforementioned existence's of foreshadowing convalescence in inspiring humanity to be conscientious and resolving to God's holy word and word's.

Patiently we must strive to live as we would not want ourselves to because pluralistically the unfathomable amount of illumination in reason cannot foreshadow enough Gaul, to even as its meaning is incomprehensible, ever be unknown to the pluralistic absolution of inspiring and exasperating one's soul. Even in asking of why retribution the thinking is not all unapparent, like the process of making a baby shows with time an understanding, so shall the existence be pained for that which its existence shuns in its own right. This truth cannot be anymore realized than the truly remarkable aspect of being brought together with the good or unrighteous; because possibly we are not in good reasoning abiding in ourselves righteously in any other way than the depiction of projecting through the eye of the untold. This feeling is much like what is within reason to abhor or acquiesce or aspire with a relative recompense to absolve our naming of anything. That for once this idea has meaning, and in this idea meaning will conclude an elucidation that compares immortality to posterity so that even in a common congruence do we even find the answer of why life is abundant, and quite simply it can only be projected as it is unknown to know the reason why except by living by good commandments.

Ever in finding does the susceptibility release all the indefinite uproars that are to be loved and enjoyed with due measures of successive proportions in prevalence? Even in direst visions can there be found good because it regulates the properties of ideals that wise men and women held to for the infraction, that justice may prevail and prevalence may abide. Even though progress in prevalence may seem slow it can appease the convalescence of aspiration because it loves itself. No person would say otherwise than the factual assumption is the mother of all fudge ups; because what reality would be real if it did not have our names as a price for which it lives and even so that this endeavor be unrelenting to aspire luscious immediacy. It can be a thirst hearty and found as misinterpreted and not reproving because of its naturalistic qualities of convicting dutifulness of ulterior motifs from which spurs envy. Not only does absolution condone this it is ever more apparent that our Gods and Goddesses are so finely interwoven with historical monuments of knowledge and appellation that it cannot be more apparent than to love these precipices. Through the chaos shall assume prosperity like the endeavor of tantamount it shall ever prelude to abide by its rules and principles. The precision of which its nature's provides can be a heart aching effect as it acquires momentum of congruent seedlings to sprout to become a fig, then branches, then a tree; and it is evermore so illusive like a Paul bearer at a wedding unforgiving and absolved like inequalities in algebra; to the forceful right that I aspire and to live to rebel against the law which I find no cause, an ever more resuscitation of actualizing our progressive nature like nature would have it. Perceptually, the idea or word has in its own right the perceptibility of being actualized with its power and manumit of providing life's sustenance in helping the lost souls onto a path of commonality. Although even though being unsure of innovation what harm would a little reform hurt in the distancing factors that lower the dilapidation of excluding constituting conceptions as means or reasons could any diligence's worth and severity abide in concession.

Precisely, the illusion of doing something unorthodox is no more wrong than committing murder for whom have you hurt, and by what means would be the less if a person was a given a choice. Absolutely, I and you must acknowledge that our own infatuation of beauty is an ever illusive victory to overcome evil because who is the wiser by what is said other than body language. The dignity of lucent perpetuality is liked for atoning to prevalence to congruent fortunes that befall in accepting the fragile applications of concordance's in conscientious terms toward pleasantness bliss.

But from the notion would it be ill conceived to elude the fact that reality would not conceive as an unobtainable dream for the mere figment of wanting it now and not knowing how long it will prolong over time through the workings of nature? Where about shall we unconsciously perceive the diligence of our fathers who knew not what they spoke but that they only knew it was appeasing for others to hear that in the involvement of its acceptance did it propitiate the substance of eternity and time, and it no longer concluded absolution of foreseeing? This I believe is the thing in which I am after to behold and to be loved by the masses so that my endeavor shall not be in vain for what other purpose shall I have than wanting to be a reputable man to everyone and in that find my meaning, my manhood, my time, and my life. It only concludes in the illusive time of acknowledging that the most efficient means of growing wiser is free thought writing that God's susceptibility can contrive but it is through his succession that we are able to acquire knowledge.

I wonder how our indefinite conscience can conspire to articulate a founding depiction in life's unexplainable subtleties; such that our prominence of oratory be self-absolving and real in contextual matters of arbitrarily seniority? Suppose for an instance we have uninvited measures which no due process could conceive to articulate our asinine passivity of duplex or the subtle acclimation of osmosis in inferring reverence. If so, this idea cannot aspire or attune for the malignant features of society like it had no disarray or convolution, such that we adhere in a manner liking to a total foreigner, but with only the thought that we must at least teach the presence of stupidity, in arranging atrophied dignitaries for their honor and disarming of arms? And nowhere conclusively could it ever be thickened to an extent that our joy is not dissolved into crevasses of perpetuality. Purposively, our endeavor is not to learn but to teach, for the purpose is illusive, the aspect evermore disheartening and ever so urgent to explain the necessities in propriety to divulge our ultimate urgency to stipulations of life. Though just as much as we need, so it can be more profuse for which the arbitration is a likeness of artificial reasons to have the clearest mind of all that would be as one.

Just like our names cannot subsume its natural existence, so shall the founding fathers absolve our plight with a degree of susceptibility that we only have life and in it even more can be found to always be incomplete and grasping for the wind. Like an absolving hierarchy of our fine figure alludes our figment of associating our fragile affirmations; as it is the cause of eluding our factions to resolve with the desire to capture, conspire, and atone the existential causality of teleology. But even in our reasoning aspects could there be anything more unreal than asserting in the caretaking of congruent factors, that living is as how life appears to be fluent and acceptable in terms of justifiable and righteous actions? Just as we can smile and constitute direction; the duty must presume without any conclusive transparency of trying to convolute the truth that there is no God; that even in him can there be resolve or in him can there be peace, for what or any other means can we conclude without a reason of doubt that the true deception be any other than what we are accustomed too is reality and customs?

Must everything be unreal and fragmented that the importance be so undone and contestant of the protruding aspiration so the dissolution truly absolve associations which are as, and can be, reformed? But just exactly how is our fortune's to contest the absolving of our life's lesser ideals by being more or less than wanting to be informed; such that the mixture, love, and concordance be resolving in the evolutionary forethought of reputable distinctions in aligning with all the realms of possibilities, and even more so to the time of relinquishing. Properly, even in us the very idea is that nothing can be for no one and no one cannot have as much as they want; so from that perspective it is convoluting our aspect of restitution, such that any endeavor is wrong and not constituting change.

Reasonably, the illusions of the Pharisees were no more apparent than the figment they thought they had on controlling the masses. It is ever so apparent that life be controlling and no one love but for the purpose of organizing the masses into a frenzy to carry out the plan that there is none. To find the fine line of causality is not its effect but more of its meaning and pillar by which it stands convoluting the orderly conviction of common concepts to pursue reason.

Does the duty of the sovereign probate the effective authoritarian evolution of subsuming intellectual processes worthy of actualization? Does the oratory of exception prose the naturalistic conception of illusory? Clearly, the thought process behind its expression can be neither exposed nor examined for simple facts of chaos; for the purpose and exposition is not to confuse but more so to hide the intent by which it is pursuing indifference in affirmations. Even though our conscience be strained it is no more self-evident than a clear figure of manumit; in all its possession, the forefront of fanaticism. Now shall our digestion proceed to endeavor into an existence of perpetuation in dispensationalism? And could it be any more real than the insight of truth to the highest peaks of wealth and health, could it possibly conceive in its own existence as a fervent misnomer that had not lived to its full progression as an insistence. Shall we proceed with the illusion that we all know, in respects to wealth and knowledge that our own mentality would not know the true nature of what it possessed. In example, a baby has no clue exactly what it wants because it is limited in the affirmation of conscience, but we being grown still lament that our existence is not self-worth in dispensation. Though the time eludes our reach so shall it extend its common assessment as to why we are here and for what purpose; and like any retroaction our own founding guidance of illusory shall feed the path of acceptance, shall dictate the absolution of dissection in parts. Like any absolving familiarity, it can congest the fulfillment of complex beings that are self-absorbing for satisfaction of conspiring to evolve to a natural existence of common psychosis. Shall we expend the outlook as an ever inclusive atrocity like any programmable function or shall we decide that the lesser the ideal the better; for even in this our minds are misconceiving such as astonishing a figment that totally does not relent to an absolution of just how everything comes together in a common bond of good. The Heirosites love their gold, the Amorites love their women, and all I love is the common good. And not to overstep my bounds but as a person I find no delight in that which I think is far off and not compiling for the fragments of my mind. I do not disorderly conduct surveys so that I can reaffirm my outlook I merely reverberate the outlook of my own name; so that I can appease the masses, for what could be more fun, to be unknown, dilapidated, and disorderly with the conduct of aforementioned prominent-hood of reasoning with truth.

I wonder if an amazement of thinking is simply a conquest of breathing; to be totally absolved in the figment of a disorderly conduct that neither blights nor congests the commonality of aberration for conscience. As we think it is not us or how is it something yet unknown to be the thought behind its thinking; the truly illusory of exception I shall proceed with enough fulfillment to feed the world over twice; it will be my founding father and I shall be like as an unconscious-able flock of wild geese; that my wings may fly higher than the heavens and never come down and it shall be like the insistence of a child beckoning to be loved. And to the extent to be heard but to never really know but only in that it was yours before it became a realistic ideal such that the world clamored to a non-existence, and truly proclaimed heaven on earth. But just like in any dissension we are mere forms consciousness absolving ideals as that perpetuates an ever inclusive realism to a Godhood, that only in the heat of the battle should any failure befall our questions. And even if we are no more right than the pillar of reason which stands to correct the assortment of eluding formative years of congressing the fictional illusion of solidarity where no allegoric reasoning can be found which we still have the acquisition of presuming we do in fact know something of perception.

Does the depreciation of consequences really take away the truth it is propounding to congruence of logic? Do our lesser ideals really have the tumult to be apprized and real? Does anything sound more absurd than the afterlife of congestion in a world of arbitrary flux of people, numbers, and money? Do you and I see that life is to be unknown in common conception of transcendence, like its discrepancies can only correlate the profession of the disciplined disciple in action?

It would seem as though we did not know of reason because of its impeccability that a lifeless artifice cannot behold the measure of organizing aggregates; such that in our lives the truly reputable are too bewildered and befuddled with an essence of pluralistic standings in a plenitude of matters. And even when we abide, we do we not get reprimanded for the forethought of existential burning of providence; the truly bidirectional insistence in a fool liking to be arbitrary in a conviction that allurements of our dignity is not be in question. Though the need would thus suffice to assist in our austere sense that is truly impenetrable in its induction and pronouncement of gains as subtle factors of contrivance in living, as is applicable as

41

an appearance of all evidence and reliance allows us to freely have an existence with pure practical truth. But even so the diligence cannot behold the profitable nature that convinces us of our energy's of time's past. To know the fulfillment in life is congesting time's progression to elude ourselves in many different ways, as such the conviction to concur of our retribution in knowledge forth wit with the dissection of conspiring to the unknowns is the reason this path is so difficult to live. For the effort is no more accumulated than an effort of constituents conspiring to level a playing field; like a rabbit or a dragonfly each has their own receptive capacities, as individual necessity's of prefixing the dissertation in a preamble of living life as though there is none. Now it makes no never mind to behold something only to lose it; for what effort would absolve liveliness and not make it right, and is there an attribution in the philandering of subsequent chapters that provide the necessity to behold in the bearing of arms? That even in our existence can this disorientation truly be revived to a heightened affect that convicts no mind; and the mind is one and the effort is one and no subtleness will change even in the transparency of evolution in asserting reason. And no abiding can be secure because of our scarcity of chains trying to break free but only die in the effort yet it was a choice; and neither can you or me convince you otherwise that the true perpetuality confines a natural existence in pan-handling the subtleties of producing prosperities or irreversible confessions of illicit fervor in congruence to time and life.

Do we conceive something other than the posited affliction in its subsuming realities of perturbation and even more do our talents apprize the serious dialect of confusing the intuitive nature of subservience to precipice? Perfectly, subservience can conceive a dualistic, idealistic contraception that even in the hour of need our diligence shines as though it was gone and totally not conceived in constituting the necessary means of obstinacies; and that our causes do not reflect any maleficent of curious ascension, but in some instances propriety will expose the association of living an acquiesced life? But even though the prominence of our picture can be more clear with fortunate obstacles obstructing the perforation of actualities confidence, as even goddesses love they cannot tame a wild nor apprize a conscience. And even in my misery the conclusive atrophied depicts the ordinance of pre-forming a lavish livestock of congruence in surviving. But where will I go that I did not realize I went because of ingenuity of the caustic matter of absolving; like I did not like or love the aspect that made me as an apparent figment of inconclusive depicting of realties convalescence. Though just as much as we reprieve or ordinate the senses relinquishing them cannot be anymore alive or real than the thought that I do not exist, yet I have no clue if I do. And so the masses praise ingenuity but is it sustainable to be alive and combine the forth right attitude that likes my name or yours for the mere thought of absolving. Shall I not like myself because of absolutions infatuation in natural convalescence to orientate evolution of good?

Yet even though we be apprized shall it be right or conducted in a fashion appropriate for God? Shall it be not convicted because it loves not what it wants but in its wants to conspire to elucidate the vision of the ordinary? Do I just want an aspect more than I want of conscience because of mere susceptibility in conclusive anthology of formative aspirates? Even in me, do I decide to dictate that attribution in an aspiration is to an effect to elude aspects such as fine figures associating reason? Just exactly how often would our life's like the truly reminiscence of grossing a figure of translucency like it was the cause that caused effects to probate congressing recompense. Would we even in the plight of our highest intrigue be able to depict dereliction of composing realities convalescence; or is the arbitrary aspect without reason and it could not sustain from the figments which seem to be so appeased and convicted, in our minds, to matters of reputable seclusion of reality? But by any means do we like or absolve the deception of its actualizing just as to how our causes, within, have a relative respect, confounded in natural ordinances such as recompensing truth. Just even in our most unrealistic conceived conceptions can our dutiful love, love our abstinences because of illusions bewildering and befuddling the translucent nature of arms, like a perception of causality in finding true founding conviction toward epitome.

Did we not have that which we already wanted to have? For which shall we be convinced that we are immortal, that our ways are right? That even in indignation do we have standards? That only in giving do we live by a bipartisan do we like? To the former, I shall not like or oblige but only in the figment of restitution shall I like; because in what possibility shall we find ourselves, in what pretense are we to be alive and in what common allegoric setting of absolving futility; and can we convince ourselves, that we have a destiny that is something without love, and of what importance of acting out that we do not care or that we show recompense for fortitude? What are we going to tell ourselves about hell that it is intolerable or unreasonably unreasonable, clearly our effectual ratio of God and death must reconstitute rationale. Contemptibly, we are told irrespectively that constituting referendum is unreasonable and that the concoction of duty and contrivance relate in such a way as to appropriate measures and coincidences of immeasurable importance; as a flame needs a spark an entire assortment of unruly reasons need the fulfillment of congruence and time.

What is not authoritative in conscientious debilitation cannot exceed proper judicature in the idea that no human can possibly know in affiant preserving by complicated conviction in ascertaining stability in life and spirituality. Because I mean really, has not God given us our due reward as it pertains to an affixation of need and want? That there be no reward for life after death such that the very meaning is not absolvable or translucent such that our entire morality be in accordance with a picture of true serenity which is desirable of any effectual mean. And like anything in time it must be preconceived as an intolerable aspiration such that our own character be on the line for our progression toward total absolution; such that our times be dissolved and no remnant of bad or good be attached to the properties of which propriety of an ethical reality that progresses to make us whole. Even if we had no mind of the absolute good, shall at least we try to succeed in our labor; such that the world be all perceivable as the world would have never thought and yet no immortality cannot be seen, and only the idea of good and absolution resound propitiation for servile confluence. And who other than the proper respects could consciously concede the energy of such affirmations that it would seem evil to be any other way.

Deciding just as to how or why our minds are online is because even in the afterhours of dreaming are, are dreams any more not real and meaningful. This is what is seeming to be the pensive passivity of unoriginal articulation that contains the propriety of translucent activities that are in themselves an introspection of dualistic meaning; and just like any ordeal this dictation can confide in dissolving prominence of the unethical orientation of leveling in our minds. Though much can be explained and preceded by a relative relatedness that conspires to the illustrious affinity to why these idealistic natures transpose ideological factions in an inexplicable resolve for impudence sake. And though even in the induction of concocting the absolute assessment dignity aspires, desires, purposes, and philanders that no parity can conclusively project other than we are not knowing. Because even in wanting can we appropriate a language such that our inner being could be no more than our outer being; and any convalescence be dissolved, because just as we want it is an unreasonable equivalence in an unrealistic fraction of desire to assist in actuating a contemptible resonance of lifting morale in all proclivity.

Like anything in reasoning with an ideal of the mind do we become stronger than the masses or mob to converse with a total being of transparency; and like any inception would it be beneficed profusely through the idea of admiration? And is it conversely actuated through the conduct of a net or hunter's weapon, within relative respects to having meaning and wisdom by which guides the mind through treacherous perils of abnormality? Though just as we will our minds so we concede actuality and though there can be no care; can we not reprieve, just like injustices that have no tail or the diviner who has no meaning, so our existences do not replicate passing our breathe. But would there be any reason to be advised that the duty which provides care can we have as much as we want and only this is a means to an end; and by any faction, would our true capabilities be any different if in them they had no meaning towards an everyday awakening of reason. How shall we transpose an affirmation if in the whole masses had neither the delight or restitution that is neither appeased or esteemed or profitable that anything could possibly exceed a testament of will; if in reason, this transposes higher than an ordeal in reparation of conscience, other than, in times reason have no need to exist to be totally content with realism? And I or you must not hate, and this can only be found in a solitude so identified with aspirants that even the universe could not hold its preeminence of righteousness.

Productively, we must provide our own necessities which are so conducive to true metaphysics that metaphysics would confide in how much we need to produce the balancing; with a respect to livelihood and definition to loquacious pondering in idealistic amazement. But even so, as much as we try to mix our character with all reasonable knowledge and traits, it must be preconceived that in its incorporation we be more absolved to the fact it is, within all reason, not just an opinion. Properly, I would have to admit that even though we are not all attune to right, the things that influence us the most we should reason an effectual state of mind. Any means can be necessary and even though what is not perceived can just as easily be as already done; so it's from this prediction that our solitude of solace rest in the aspect of our life; which is fond and fluent in entreating illustrious intrigue of moral profit. And if any other conviction be absurd or out of place it still has the thought that in its acknowledgement a true reality is congesting to be aspired, disposed, and resolved through the natural evolution of time, space, and matter.

Reasoning to become as an incipient, is not as far-fetched as the ideal of our lives transpiring our natural existence in various tumults. And even in no clearer cause could there be such justification for actualizing the capabilities which are strewn together as waves crash an obstacle; and it could not be clearer if in any ordinance of assimilation be unequivocal to artificial genealogy in excitement. And even though I care must I live, and even though the inoculation of a perspiring reprove to acquiesce aspirants; and could any clearer dilapidation confide in the idea that true prosperity of us could be more short lived because of time, though it has meaning and figures of expressive continuity, it has to have the meaning as to why we are here; and any figment of either of the two be totally not heard and only in the refinement of learning would it be plausible to conjugate ruling? The more I seem to interject myself the more I wonder, "how so, or why," and just as we find ourselves could things become within attainment or even in good belittle that which is right as to appropriate our ingenious scheme to steal and plunder the very good souls who are clueless to its affects; yes or no is all there is but even so the most monstrous of the question," What is real?," is never to say it, and to be sincere and articulated of rendering of how it affects us, and to the point which we will make it affect others. And just as to how we are to find ourselves is no more puzzling than a mean that produced something other than was feasibly thought; and it cannot attest to the consignment by which it is imposed and lamented in conducing us to believe that the world has the answers.

What shall we have to realize an effectual propriety? Can we not love and in loving our knowledge behold better? To be higher than any natural existence to conspire the forthright of adulation in conception is reasonable in its ascension as it appears fluent and conscientious in our own meanings as we learn as they allow us to understand our own lives. But even in our aspirants it is untried or constructed to extend of natural perpetuality through an example of unconscientious predilection in never unending. And even so, could my dislike of misfortune habits concede to preclude dominance with the ordeal that even knowledge's deal will always be higher even if we have more than anyone. I am in coexistence such that the prospect future convolutes reality, as one conspiring to ventilate the thalamus by which our inoperable predilections are redirected to the promulgation of consensus in disciplining and teaching citizen's truth. And even as much as we would like expose our own endeavor; and in the forethought, perceive by which it is pensive and absolving, but through our progressive ordeals could the aspirations taunt the objective destination, to superiority, of knowing and inferiority of acceptance of true honesty.

Should we concede that we are no better than the thoracic individuality, like it matters if we care or not, like an own individual suicide of soul like we never existed and in this ideal what would have us as explicably reliant of acquiescing our reality, the reason that accepts all conscience. And even wondering can it arbitrate our possessive inquiry of natural sustenance, by the predilection of conspiring through illusive means which have no clearer ideology than the substance which it is said in a presumptuous attenuating to dividing abidance of austere. Just how much can we live and not care, to ever to be by ourselves through the total tantamount of indicted to the process of uninvolving natural prospects to faceless amorality. Shooting the prospect of professional ominous and unequivocal connotation, like it wasn't through an adulate duality conveying a system through the revering ordinances of proof in innocence. Just how are we to come to an affirmation if aggregating factors that have not the refinement of frantically concocting to the elevating aspirants; like any individual has the knowledge to dictate a truth that is just a shadow of the aforementioned delirium. But just what is good, real, and not absolving that its induction did not care to behold the naturalness of omniscience; the idea cares not for which it can comparably compares to the laws of constraining and refraining from convoluting the reprimand of an actual ordeal by which convalescence confesses adolescence of discipline. Even I hate not like a somebody just ordinary fellow with the most good to perceive and revive and just love; why would I not curtail the dutifulness of perturbation to the disposition of confabulating a lucidity attracting confidence, and can I live and not do just in introspection or avarice to congruent commonality in trapping the stones of peoples souls so that drowning oneself in the worlds sorrow no longer assist in the tantamount of unoriginal pacification of endless and unfruitful talk.

Through thorough examination, of a dogmatic life in the mind, I have found in the causation of sensible worth, there is nothing as orgasmic by concluding that the intellect, judgment, and reason are our pleasers and if anyone tell you different they are a fool. Though just as examining can be perceived so can an artificer of the different indoctrinations of a causal way, the interloper, the profounder, the dignitary, and the artifice, and even the will of doctrinarians in the absorption of aspirants and adherents in pathology, assume evanescence in the prospect of our lives changing for the better as all reality begins to change. In as amusing as this sounds, how the imperceptibility to be found in contesting the articulation of absorption such that there is the cause and the artificer, as time is present, so l always assume there is something attending to the consonance of human faith. This whole total superiority, is what artifact am I possessing, yet is nothing, but the evolution of understanding casual manners and even this is lacking in the assumption that life lives as it apprizes consonance. And this makes you think, is the spice anymore tastier than it once was, if in consonance of all practicality there are many spices that attribute to many tastes? And who shall be our approvers, the law and in its own right in the idea of a capitalistic market for not all of us but have the ingenuity and self artificer for a good home and right decisions and even in the artifice can anything be clearer? And the self sounding tone of appropriate manners shall be of the ego and in this I approve the dereliction of commodity. And by who shall adulate the effective nature of cause and unsound intuitiveness; the artificer has no need for will, or absorption, or passion; it is all on the convalescence that one day we are to die or will God make us a relict as he did Adam and Eve.

Clearly in this we are misperceiving the artifice in any or apparent aspiration or even in the actualization can there be assigned a preeminence of godliness, as to the ideal the actualization of self-preservation relates in a concerted commodity. And no less or more could a more conclusive endeavor behold such an aspiration and the foundation of a superstition absolution; by a very conducive infatuation with imperceptibility as a reasonable idea; that as we like, it will life progress; but could the need of adoration and fondness be in-line with the perception that even in carelessness does our true recognizance exceed even those things which are as like anyone else to be such that our oration is exponential in the depiction; this the true valor or gluttony that lies not in the world, but is the world, in the soul contesting to be alive and reprieved without judicature of force or consequence of failure or success.

The thing with any endeavor is not so much how you get there but how you convict the time and effort through philosophy or reading to depict the oration of rhetoric and knowledge; and even in any endeavor that our true incipient being is not like a man, or woman, but is a total fool and cannot be called anything else for our wanting to please, and not have the dereliction of conducing our needs because of thinking, as in time, it is truly apparent that any and all is, is the true meaning behind the dereliction of actuality of recompense, or how they say in Buddhism, the way. And can anything be more apparent or loved such a fact that the only dignitary would reprove ratiocination in the natural existence of love and good. But even in our absolution can any artifice be depicted with a pronoun such that it be unheard or wrong when really neither matters except that of the true avocation. This, I find no more amusing than an unsung gallantry transposing to fight another demon; to do right in God's eye's, but though, in concept, good is bad and bad is good so from that perspective who are we to rely on; the senses, the individuality, the convalescence, or the aspiration, yes they give the mind words of oration but the true pigmy of life is that of letting it pass by as Epictetus would say.

I myself am no better than the beggar because just as Socrates, I am a gadfly to the masses because I believe true perceptibility can never be found until after death or until a world without it is better to preserve and extend our own souls from perturbation of convalescence, in conceding and extruding the figment, by which is the true natural calling of a predecessor of intelligence. And no one shall leave unhanded or absolved but the true indoctrination that will be dissolved and not concocted to the point that frailty extends its worth or shall any individual know this; or be absolved by the dignitary which is truly bestowed to a convalescence of liking or not liking; but what tragedy should our own perception be changed by retribution of the pigmy of the infidel and not love and abhor consignment of truth. The dignitary of the true life is the name I will not even call because I am imperfect and just like any individual I am striving for my likes and dislikes; and even though I dislike I love and extirpate convalescence. And even in bewildering the truth of perception the doctoring of knowledge cannot live a lie and will not absolve or love because it makes no sense being under the seat of judgment and lying in between because it is influentially perturbing the fallacious fixation of elemental futility of trying in earnest. And this perceptible truth must be of the absolute affixation because even in liking do we or do we not transpose ourselves apprized to the task of the absolute ridiculing ourselves because of our manhood and our genitals. Why else shall there be persistence and even trying to interpret with an acknowledgement of sufficing to deprive the natural essence of restitution, by which is the true destination of aspiring or just being in-line with prudence; so with this in mind I am truly understanding that a true dignitary must absolve priori's; and even in these instances we must absolve the true naturalness of liking to have heart and bestow sound theology of ethical propriety.

I must conclude there is no ostentatious absorption of perpetuality that does not integrate the fine figments of natural occurrences; even caustic actuality disproves the existence in an artistic aberration in the anomaly that allows anyone to live, just as trying to inquire into propriety can one confidently be commiserated. And any reasoning aspect is conductively the aspirant of an individual through a convolution which is copasetic by propitiating an authoritarian admiration; which professes in profuse extending attributes that any clear understanding individual can affix conglomerating rules. But prophesy is like any individual conspiring to correlate an effective nature by any clear consciousness by comparing it to an apparatus in a truly resolving idealistic commode ration of precipice. Though like anyone I ask can a true amount of knowledge ever perspire any effect that conductively conspires to adulate occurrences in resonating a social recognizance in an actuality that abides by a reasonable aspect of conformity; yet I ask not but a bridge to the thinking that reality's possession is an articulate commodity that is not seen as too impulsive, or recoiled through unfamiliarity that neither composes to actuate a progressive transformation of liking or disliking common causes.

Are we, being, itself a rectified in the thalamus of connectivity and an instituting depiction of authenticity rightfully imposing a transient involvement in measuring catatonic's; by which a restitution can be alleviated toward a victory of imperialism; and this in its meaning is the focus in any individual market, but what by any precedent would actuate the material of Protestantism; and even as how or why the reasonable response is to be self-disposed in a determination of appealing to God in the idea that he is still wiser and any journey of his is never over. To be as if nothing was real and the only thing that matters is the self absorbing factor that absolves a truly fictional character; and who or why would it be unrelenting with a common causality that occurs through a consecration of ideals. The true meaning may be a dream, an illusion with only the sense that it is as being blind in 3 different planes of ourselves in the idea that true prodigality of adoration is the affixation of absolute pathology.

And just as how we are almost surprised to make claims that just as it can be seen unrelenting with associating all the realms of reality through a natural preponderance which we acknowledge that are truly alive; and what better involvement can we decide or aspirate in transcending our consciousness of formulating a plan or deciding not to live but only by ideas which are needed and formed because of arrogance and ignorance yet in true strife virtue must be always be in our minds.

Then even as we construct our thoughts in a formation towards impenetrability the sustenance of life abides by no other ideal by the pure-resounding aspiration that true love is no love and even in our resolution can this be a more truer contradiction, yet still acknowledging, to be opposing to the aspect we are all alone. Nowhere is there true love like incandescence. The abstainers are beholding true realism and like any importance can a more concessive proclamation be bestowed with a remnant of sociology truly be reached if our lives are anymore involved in actualizing substantial's (substance); the relativity transpires to new ideological ideas that contract our necessary mental faculties of reputing, not acting, in prudence yet irreconcilable to true progress. Even in our unrelenting causation, where else shall it be, in composing effortless connotations with the hope of truly propitiating a conviction, even unseen, though acting on an idealistic commonality we must be transacted in an absolutely unconventional way that even as we are directing could an existence be so appalled or predisposed to articulate affirmations from conclusions which have no premises; and only want to be absolved because of a heightened individuality in that the more we predicate, the more our selection of propriety expands.

Eventuality makes sense because even as our successors will carry a golden staff for the improvoso(a word I like to use as an existence fathering another), and engage to precipitate a cavern of aesthetic comparison for pessimistic appeal and concern. And no benevolent character will not act more than the perceptual character of abstracting convalescent-subservient imparities in invigorating matters of absolutions as in composites relate some sort of complicity as we begin to see our journey. This pertains to individuals who can reason in copasetic condoning of heavenly-charismatic purities that absolute resounding realities representing nations of thought; because just as many people are alive and dead can any clearer consciousness be appealed than the hierarchy of dimensions, through ever inclusive fortune's, that appertain to prevalent levels of intellect. And even as we invoke perceptive solidarity we impose with respects to any medium the artificial imparity that reasons rarity, by being more enforced in pervading disassociation of constructing, through enforcement, to abstract plurality in actuating differential matters through rigid palpitation of the psyche's conscious steps toward vagrancy. Though in our fragmented incapacities (echelons) insistently profound, in consistence in a reasonable disposition will allow our timing to be involved with conscientious debilitation on aggregated ideals; in that no possible mind can possibly conceive with only the consciousness that it does abhor a natural affixation toward concordance of being prude to congruent normalcy of echelon austerity.

In any of our conquest we must convict, as clear as day, the natural essence's of humanity because forevermore love is an infatuation of knowledge and dilapidation. And in our most cohesive endeavors that is all they are and in any instances can love arbitrate a conviction which even absurdity can cure? Promptly, our desire for love or attenuation cannot console the reputable difference between a love that is knew it was not perfect and one that is so mysteriously abounding, in that it cannot love anymore, because of mere unforgivable rights of being unlawful to one thing that meant the world of propitiation in conscience and plurality to convict idealism. I cannot attest to something I do not love, nor abhor by the infractions and pain it has caused me; and because of mere fervor, I care not because in the reasoning of the idea it can only care that I do not live and even in dilapidation am I truly known; for it is for the cause of knowing and not caring and I abhor both, why I do not know. And for what prospect am I doing that I care not for my own and that any endeavor would be futile if I did make the mistake to care; shall I only love what I know and feel and even in the endeavor not care at all. For what propitiation, am I to like and what absolvent nature shall contract the things which had no care, because like any idealistic man it is erupting to find that this is the only means by which we can put into practice the percept of actualizing nature and our conscience.

Why should any of us conclude that we do care when in reality it is nothing except selfish desire of self and appeasement; and it cannot abhor or prolong an effective resolution by which any figment would be unreal of absolute sincerity that even God has no nature; because what is good of self-absolving a love that did not care or to have a point only to dissolve it and it totally disappear forever.

In this instance, it pisses me off that I can care and that I do not love for the sake of just loving; because nothing else matters when it comes to the true account and testimony of a neighbor, which could be no truer than a gigantic ant eating a human. So I shall not care or like within a retribution which even God does not know because truly he is infinite but like any flaw unable to be human; it is only in us that he is and because of this I am ever more pissed off, to where I want the world to end and my life to end because I have no love for what you love; you only care to inoculate yourselves with desire and ambition and I will have no part of it because I am a man. Like anybody you should care that I take pity on you appealing to your senses and ever wanting more of an aspect that is not myself and I shall only do what I am told and no one shall be the wiser.

Like a pontificating infidel do I understand and absolve because I know love and attest that I do know the frantic prediction of worldly consolation; and nowhere like myself shall I be any more clear than thinking that I did not, and for insistence on our principle's can the truly triadic visionary inoculate slumber by which I am so scared that I have wronged my God in any way and that I have no clue of time or godliness only that I wish to understand that which I do not know. And in these visions I can have as many or all subconscious realities that deduce a natural causality by which I do wish to know and what forefront will you have me; what God shall you have me worship or what dignitaries butt should I kiss. These are as any what I abhor and hate and all you can find the time to say is do I love, do I not care, you know what I have to say to you, is you know not what you do, and without corrective reproof we have nothing to gain and nothing to lose, so it is out of this endeavor that I say be at odds and never say: "I am ever to give up or go out of life unknowing," for the unknowing always know something.

And where shall we go in an ever illusive endeavor of strife and matrimony of the contesting absolution of taste. And am I not appealing, do I not make the remnants in your mind asunder, does anything seem a right and practical to synthetic pretenses? And it is only this that I can find time for because writing is the only thing that I have that is true and worth something to my you and me. Even more so in the dereliction of time and inoculation with a probate to matter would it not be concise to say that I do hate or abhor a manner which neither loved me or cared for me because everyone has seen what I have become. And can you know or help or entice to entrap a person in the confinements of a prison cell to make them err in their ways; and shall any opposition abide or care that even as we see there is no other retribution but the confines of living apodictically. Who can protect my rights other than what I wanted protected, can you concur with an ever illusive figment in consuming just as to how one is to live and forthright with a time coming. You cannot console my artifice, artistically who can, me or you, neither, so let's let it be that a true person is one whom like me knows a time will come when I am to be dead and no one can convince me otherwise except by the fiction of my own mind.

Why must we acquire a natural talent of self absorbing perpetuality and even in its succulence can it be any farther from the right or the dereliction of pursuing just as to how we come by an artifice of consistent oration. This explains why, I do not do as all would presume to hate as much as I do because prophetically it is abounding in self love and loathing in reputable acts of superiority; and by this fiction can we conceive any other, that this percept absolves a natural translucency of arbitrating a congressional hearing of absolution. But do we care when we put the waters to the wind and in insistence could life be any clearer in perpetuality by actually conceding to a natural confounding that is an ever illusive reality of pigmentation of forgetting and actuating life's lessons in prodigality. Even in our time the days cannot as they are be suspected by a duty that completely misses a mark or aspires higher than planes that naturally coexist with convalescent imparity of reputable attribution. And even in the minuscule of its expression could any appropriation decide just as to how matter shall collide, shall we leave that area to God; or should we by pontification acknowledge that we are alike with causes in an appropriate manner. Why do you misconceive that I hate, and that I only care that I have time with a natural translucency which I absolve as my time has come; and by any aspiration can a clearer conception of involvement truly apprize an affixation on a convalescent attitude to a man and math that truly arbitrates a correct path. But by the same token the lesser we converge on translucent terms there is more unclear consciousnesses that try to abhor and artfully impose in life's consistency through matters of arbitrating a logical and outspoken natural existence?

Though with a percept toward the indefinite or an ever illusive conception of artfully imposing on our factual evidential passivity, can a clearer and concise idea be realized; through actuating natural persistence is not apparent that any clearer reality naturally articulates juxtaposition through professed alterability of opposites. But why must we lie, it is as if, we do not see the reality towards which we are arbitrating a concise attribution which is good and self proposing to a world of unimaginable exasperation. And just as we associate through aspirations which no needle in a haystack could confirm that, we as, a dignitary could not abruptly arbitrate a cause or the cause. And we are just as appeased as you anyone fulfilling dreams and realties which we neither care because truth in apparel of functions to be unrealized and just as to how it concocts a natural evolutionary-distillery of reasoning is beyond conception. Because even as we care there could be no cause which was not truly in-line with an attribute of causal insistence that did not love and abhor just as to how we can care, and can we find any more time not to know? Thoroughly a time must come when I will leave and only in time and in the present can there be any more subtlety that I love and find it good; because just as to how it is, is because it is and in that finding can a probate acknowledge and know our dereliction or self. But through our congruent matters there has to be more that we like and absolve, and by a reality can we ever more appear as unknown in a natural concurrence of methodical attenuation. But just because we can do not make it any more unreal than a time of actuating our ancestry history of knowledge and those times of heartache and time; and it could not be any clearer with a mindset that abhors a natural time of convalescence. But by anything do we abhor even in times of unnerving orderly pessimistic arbitrary attribution of collecting and composing them in all its perpetuality of infertile times of having grace and knowledge to coexist as each was something we did not know. But by thorough reasoning can any idea truly absolve a naturalistic quality than neither artfully impressed visionary tactics by which it was cohesion of neither side and of nothing but in knowing nothing is the true idea and reality. A truly concise explication, must incur that our characters have no need to induce attenuating circumstances which have no need for these attenuating circumstances because like nothing these circumstances are a farther remnant of attribution to be conceived in order that we love and also that we do not.

Our minds make no sense to use because just like in the dereliction of life could any truer portrait of magnification confer on the natural evolutionary conception and process of times arbitrariness in presiding over rules and laws. Why must we know what our grace of arbitration in conduct we must assume to perpetrate the confinement of the truly supreme and imperial God or Sage and come together as all alike people and no misconception can be misconceived.

So I make a way like a lost cause, but must we assume we are not alike in fortune or fame like as a dignitary is unjustified by being beneficent for individuals in themselves; so where in the world, fluently, can we coexist that we do not love and abhor, and must we find it in ourselves or in the ways of the west. Also too, how can superiority confine us to a room of excellent behavior like it is a cause that we hated; or by what fictions do our exasperations pontificate a natural evolutionary time-synopsis of reason, only God knows and I have no idea why.

Would it be to indigent of me to abhor a friend in a time of need yet let the reputable go because I cared not for his or her time? And by any means many will say but without any dereliction I am lost and not in a time I care not for because I am only impervious to the times of grateful artifice or intellectual substratum of artfully sound consultation in living but I am out of touch with reality. And even in its most subtle subtleties could any decision be preserved with a natural essence to love and artfully compose a saunter of melancholies attributing to catatonic proficients for prosperity and propriety's sake?

Do we really know with an artifice of prosperity that even though we invigorate a destiny that even in a careless aberration could a time come more sooner than when I died. So you see my soul has died and I am merely speaking to you in the dialectic of sound reverberating in my conscience for your mind; like a time of unforgettable knowing how I forget and not realize an artifice of a natural existence which neither cares to love or abhor me because I am indifferent to externals; and even in time of cause could there be any retroactive reputable action that I or you did not like or attenuate just exactly how we are thinking and feeling? And by what of any other causality am I to like and abhor natural convalescence of attitude and judicature. Like I am some incipient foreign bean counter that just hates to abhor or attenuates circumstances by natural convalescences that are not a part of a plan that takes all and never wants anything to do with the juxtaposition in our ideals or consistencies in the living standards of how we live and how we provide for ourselves is inconsistent with having feelings. Though even the atrophy has its place and time like it always abhors and finds a judicature, for which is an exact opposite of sincerity's absolution, so who are we to believe?

Even in the sight of plurality could any concise exposition be more intuitively inclined to inoculate a reasonable amount of articulation by strict objections, can there be a relative means of actuality in asserting reason? But even so the deciding of translucency could it even in the senses not be an artifice to include a natural consistency by causes that would profitably correlate an evolution through expressing or exaggerating concise matters of exposition? Does orderly contact of eluding or concocting the formidable abilities of expedient terms, by us, by inoculating transparency in terms of good; as in any real actuality can an expressive attitude be something we did not like as an absolute argument in presuming our own fallibility? Though just as time can concoct notions and realities of immeasurable cohesion of confining a natural time by many absolute means could any ordeal not be acted? In the evidence that it did not exasperate a convolution with natural existence in an artificial congruence to uncover the susceptibility of time and cause is neither an absolute victory nor artificer that occurs in a dualistic composition of something clearly unrealized and not real. But concisely can there be a time of cause in an ordeal of naturalness in a time of reality to presuppose with a concurrence of dilapidation, in an ever successive absolution of plurality conceiving in the times of oppression be so sincerely actuated in a factual progression of convalescence?

The thinking in assorting a disposition of incurring factual avarice in the thoracic artery be impervious to imparities, can any reasoning applicability be advised in truthful absolving by deciding in the idea that no improvements shall be made in synthetic concentration? And in even liking our susceptibility could any transgression absolve our natural coexistence with perpetuating a deciding dereliction of aberration in time and reason within relative respects to duty and concession; but even in this affinity can any clearer consciousness assort the affirmation of good and conclusive purities. Though just as we are in the sight of senses can any clearer ideal aspire to planning or articulating confidence with an aberration of conception artfully conspire to predict futuristic times and post-modern analytic's, this profession is what we neither absolve or like. By congressional articulating a congruence of commonality would any aspiration like that of dignity or superiority in confidence expound a common artifice of good; so like even in this congestion of art would any sounding aberration love or behold congruence with dignity in its respects to idealism. Though as we are intrigued to behold an ideal like no other the whole adulating matter cannot consume our natural essence to absolve and love that which is totally superior to our intelligence. And like any common matter a truly unreasonable character cannot assume and behold the care which loves and beholds the tendencies in rebutting an absolution in time and a course of action in appropriating a line of imparity or an attribution of variant commerce.

Could any clearer association conduce us to be enthralled with a name other than that which is unobserved or conserved to an absolute superiority with conducing terms by means of actuation; of differing the thoracic in a conclusion by which our duty is ensued with associating factors of perpetuating aspirants in a successive hierarchy of orientation? But why of anything would not the aspirant absolve the aspiration in any ordeal which can conclusively be determined and absolved by an orderly cognizance. Why would our inherent nature occur with a relative force of attenuation by producing enlightenment of a complex contradiction; in an ever invisible study which evens the congestion of the imperial oratory be as if we did not think it or know through a conclusive evidence of finding a natural occurrence of art. But by any aspiration shall our time come like it is unintentionally absolving a conception of prevalence or unassisted as a just reality composes judgments by an artifice imposing the prospect of our reasoning ability of concordance to truth; but also what means can suffice a carrier confining in an aspirant of absolving just as what we think and feel and are two totally separate objects; that in wanting to behold and separate both by knowing that in the instance of absolving this idea would truly be apparent for time of recourse, which loves but is stern in the reasoning applicability of being able to segregate both and know within ones abilities to use and know one over the other.

In our absorption can any clear relativity artifice a name that clearly associates with realms of natural congruence of absolving a dilapidation of figurative improvisation that clearly exposes, explains, and exasperates a methodical resolution of time and age; to the respectability as we acquiesce and others who cannot comprehend the illusion of reality. Though just as we care could we not care in a relative reform of justice, like time had no place, and the subconscious of transcendental knowledge did not appropriate how everything fits to include order of reason. By which the terms do we associate our ferocity as a quality that has no patience or division in composition, but the pieces by which clear ideals of realty have a need with ideas of reverent aberrations to plainly assist in the affixing to atone to the universal complacence of eventuality to caustic revelry is reasonableness. This is evermore conspiring to the true destination that has no end and the truly absolves the reality of ordeals, and in the exasperation, that would concoct how life organizes through the loss of impurities by which the forethought of conceiving this is not known by reading but by mere inclusion of precipice; but only in our conscience can any clearer conception or reasoning truly aspire to pontificate the meaning of beholding a natural evolution. For even other causes have no superiority in instances of a second that succumb to allow us not to be free though we are translucent to nature's proclivity; for what superiority does our reasoning or respectability naturally induce as a concise aspirant, that like perceiving ideals, that all succumb and adulate a successful power of revelation.

By any precipitance would any actualization truly confound a motif as if it was perpetual to self subsuming veracity, by any measure can there be, unintentionally, substratum of proficiency in knowledge, that perspires to elude catatonic congruence of liveliness. Prophetically, our purpose should be to inoculate a synthesis contrary to appellation or appearance to appropriating actions by exclaiming ourselves to a predilection of obeisance or postulation, in the prospect in the future to variegate artifice. We preclude to find an associative display of indivisible waves of appeasement that there shall be a judicature that subsumes any natural existence which any plurality can obviate to attune our incandescent minds, in that any true imperial authority, could be perceived as not equal and not liked, to an aberration toward illuminating means to where our faculties of perception include reverberating our conscience to prevalence. Prosperously, we must extend an imperialist amount of adulation, such that the distancing of our reasoning and awareness alert us toward reprieving, with an inoculation in affixing resilience by, profitable means by a clear consciousness that stops and inoculates with granger. But truthfully are we being like a fly searching for that ever exclusive meal that will provide us and him with happiness because of nature, and in this essence the domination of illusive connotations correlate to affixing placement of rationale and logic.

Though times incurs much dilapidation, there is so much more that is not imposed on the ideal that our true convictions lie not in the artifice of determination but in the dereliction of time's enthralling; with absolving time to consume a true aspiration and dictation that can correlate with auspices absolution, to us, as prodigal individuals who regard essence as an attributable quality. It seems there is some sort of indivisibility that truly precludes to acknowledge that we are all one and like any other person we have flaws and convictions wanting to aspire as Christ had ascended. Though, however enchanting, in this post-modern world of dereliction we should not conceive the means of deprecation, but preclude to love and absolve the figments of our minds trivial aspirations. To interdict with an exclusive interdiction our minds can clearly precipitate measures of opposites by having in time an evolution of tantamount. It is clear from this that a reprieving duality of our conscience cares not for ill-relevant ideals in an interlocutor that assumes depictions of fluency that are incurring propitiations resolve towards contentment. Though our absolving ideals have a nature of unforgettable consolation, what truly beholds our cognizance that we reprieve and assert restituted means of goodness and badness in speculative and authoritative profession, is the ideal that all life exists as to be a means to succeed others.

Though just like anyone I am hesitant at a time to displace that which I abhor and aggregate because of futility and unimaginable reprieve in condescension, but I am naturally wanting to aspire by evolving your and my needs and aspirations as conclusive affixation to propound restitute values; or likewise that which has always been yet unseen to perturbation in straits of aberration in unison of universalism. And to aspire as we want than any ordeal must absolute a transcendental conviction that truly likes or dislikes such that in all times translucency causes that which has been and will always be a time of cause and change since there is no doubt to realities convictions in forethought. It just makes you think if any true superiority is not right because ill management which is only liked because of blackmail not because of ingenuity and justice but because of mere infatuation of cunning. Condoning to acclaim to this is something I do not believe is right because like any injustice does it truly reprieve with an ascension such that we have no cure by which you, I, or action cares not for a loss of life other than God approves any justification for the taking of a life and judgment awaits thee later on. This shows why we dictate how we live, talk and associate fluency in matter, in which neither, are as, as real as they come; because what truth in a person who has no thought or care except for the common thought that true time accelerates occurrences of ominous seniority that transcends aspirants, truth would have dictating and commanding time to absolve and adhere to the appearance of thinking for the body.

Just as, as much as can be seen, so shall a preponderance of natural advocacy help in the plurality of causes, that any of us would rather approve, of this incumbencies because of indications of affection; but like any reason can our consciousness actually convict time and space as though there is no other aspectual rationale which respires convalescent attitudes? Like any idea where can consciousness adhere and such that the reality concoct with a restitution as if it is merely the only cause which is the vindication of historical warfare. As though any ideal I have I hate and anything I absolve or behold I lose within the suspension of time do I see that nothing happens then that of the superiority of ego and aesthetics. But what is consciously absolving the thinking that reprieving aspirations contrive to coexist with fragments of past history to bestow ideals such that now is what we still see just not conclusive in terms of appropriation. Why must we not love or abhor a justification that truly beholds conscientious imperialism with a justification that time heals all wounds and in dereliction of it is actually wanting more than is needed. Even in ideals we lack for in other peoples selves do we either relent to want to be friends or imposed to other people we know, but no real good as to how it applies to logic and politics. This cannot be any clearer than in the illusion of actuating by which we are articulating with a clear resolution, like not knowing is not so absurd, as knowing but the true testament is going to be prejudice and conscientious awareness.

I never said I was not a good person that is so belligerently ill-advised by the common necessities of life; which is forbidden in the translucency that obliges myself to propitiate with; in concocting lesser extremes with a hierarchy of ideals that will shear Maslow in natural occurrence and pro-divisible aspirers like a tumult that makes me have too much time. I do not know if I will ever illusively exegete a preponderance of such self absorption that liking would ever dare challenge it; because my mere assertion to life is that I do not have and the things that our real is what God transcends or the devil does; because like any good necessity it is a must that the fluency of dictatorship must absolve the compaction of arbitrating a vindictive asshole to obliterate not just us but himself too. Why must I in the conclave of existence abide by rules which I neither care or vindictively evolve an aggregation of sorts, that totally dictates an absolute victory for nothing of myself or anyone else but by what we do not know and just how far we can get to know. Even in the midst of purity, for even this is unequivocal to a liking by which any measures of caution float in the wind of ignorance, like a true preponderance ever evolved to tell us that, "Hey you are extinguished!,"; and what you can do about it involves pain staking—mythology and lesser extents superstitions, which lead to no known agendas that masticate precarious measures of elucidating just how fiction can concoct, which will induce an outlook that any purity, even in its most astounding vigor, can still be higher. What are we doing that we are not satisfied with capitalism that our lesser ideals be totally dissected which would conduce assessments, like in an outstanding presumptuous, by which any ideal would conclusively actuate just as switching in the presence of transforming our own selves with a polarity that truly deduces; from relative cognizance that any person can truly arbitrate just as to how plane's of existence change from word to word; and the whole world in our minds have unintentionally just dissolved language and understanding to limits which neither persist to abide by relativity. Even in a junction box the word could possibly conduce an after stay night in a friendly relativity in our primordial states that any clear incipient being would naturally absolve away what I like to call, "The dying of ideals," and never more translucently would provocation be a natural occurrence to ordinate; a fine figure of association, could ever appease a person's sense for recollection, and are in complete consciousness of being something other than by which we wanted to be; but in being are we completely what we said we would not be. Because convalescence abhors and I have to acknowledged that I am stupid before the courts but like any practice it seems it can only get better; the realities of condescension, the arbitration of superiority, and the tantamount of victory by not even fighting. Where shall I go that I already did not want to be or where shall we go where there is lesser to do yet more involvement with the psyche and unlearning bullshit that has tacitly clouded our bullshit for a millennium of centuries. Occurrences just do not happen, it is predisposed and arbitrated like an aftermath which no one predicted because of shear brilliance of a system that is failing as a society. Only in a true dictatorship can people be made to feel like people when their wishes are obeyed and no one is to tell the wiser of invitations of life's past time, and a full concoction of translucent means that have no reasons because of mere fulfillment of the law. But just in eerie accumulation of congruence would any imperial outcome be truly primordial; in the absence of time, a true predilection obviate a prediction that no clearer cause in contraception's belittle the truly absolute outcome by which time in outstanding efforts would neither impose or expose what needs to be, in relevance, nothing at all.

Does true conviction come by destiny in a solution that any bipartisan could consciously conceive as an assessment of righteousness like an interjector of an aspiration; by any means does the disassociation of convalescence have an ulterior motif that in conclaves that truly construe the dominance of some impersonal civility? Though just like any ideological faction can any clearer restitution contract in its syntax in arbitrating a figurative solution that shines as causality in an idealistic nature, can this clearly absolve lunacy by which is no more unclear than the idea that true love transcends true perception. And even in vigor would I associate a common end like in pathways, would any ideal reason to aspire into conclusive evidential matters as a carelessly posterity of hierarchy or abstraction to abdicate that any measures which precludes to absolve to be unfound and not heard because of ignorance. By any inclusion would absolving be any clearer as in indecisively disposing of relativities alliance's; like a subconscious substratum of artificial power by evidence or of the unequivocal of heresy which no clearer dilapidation can artfully impose on the thought of dereliction which predisposes the ulterior motif that any indictment cannot clearly resolve or understand: For any logical fallacy is inadvertent that true honesty rely not on intuition but primordial perception that our own true love be clearly restitute in absolving by which reality is seen for its truth. Why does relativity not bestow how we favor individual serendipity would supersede that of what has always been and cannot change because the mere faculty of congruence that completely disassociates with perceptions of just how they correlate with idealistic commonality. But just as fear and envy become ever so more apparent no truly acting character can behold perfection; so that in its proclivity absolution will have a resolution to question or ask reason, and justice can succeed; for what figure would we presume to know other than selfish desires of affixation that atones for an outright unreasonable dichotomy, like we as individuals do not already have enough. Because truly how involved are we with ourselves that the dialect of retribution would not clearly dictate an absolving factors that absolutely care for a people that it cannot help but condescend like it is all out in the open and deception is not in practice. Though it is inconceivable that true nature would behold an absolution that a true dictation can only purport the faction of assessing figures of attribution which depict the associating relativity that cordially invites us as a successor aspirates; with fluency of truth even the depiction of any ideal, idea, or composition could not dilapidate the fate which can have and should have as pluralistic providential solidarity.

I wonder, and by all means I do, where can the theocratic authority arise where any impenetrability conduce our own relativity to the mastication of an atom bomb exploding into abstract art which deduces. And any clearer observation would totally aspire in an inclusive concession in the art of reposing. Though even in actuating a convalescence could a acquisition or artifice measure with the knowledge's forbearance of duty that actually archives tenacity in retributions fluently in sensation of ordeals that conclude imparity? Though just as we ordinate a concise preeminence; in artificially imposing a restituted mind to the not casual distorting visions of remembrance of citrating the providential affluent ominous excessive goal, the ideal of reason should still suffice an exegete circumstances. But even in the thicket of presuming we know not what we know we recompense ourselves with the resolution that all conclaves naturally conduce us to believe in the dark of the oscillation, to absolutely, in the vindicating of a destitute positive of polarity and sincerity repute individual conscience to precipitance. And even though in our most honest absolving factions can an aorta of indulgence contrive to abdicate atrocious superiority of actuating my name or yours; where is anything to constrain reverberation of the astute vigor like even in caring does this transpose figures of monstrosity to the aforementioned forefront of a topic of attributable resolve.

Do we love as it is unjustified in a consolation to justifying, that any ill-perceived or ill-deceived in accumulation of successive hierarchies is right; like a tether of heartache, like our reputable conscientious divulging is not acquiesced to an aberration to aspirate necessary reference? Though just as we interpret our tangents or excessive characters of appropriateness, likes a concordance of fearful effects in perceptual canals of conceptions; such that we preclude to acclimate an insistence of authority like even in our own selves it is not ours, for even in the law it is not for the lawful, but the unlawful. And even in further assertions shall our justification be absolved like any ordeal that has no cease of harassment because of a dereliction that truly reprieves by absorbing material of accumulation in rightful actions. With an insistent barrier can we possibly conceive or appease a natural affliction which neither caused nor loved an effect such that it was ill caused or loved an effect such that it neither resolved nor accumulated to a justifying principle of acceptance. Even as we cause time, can any more one instance be unseen in its appropriate conception of affluence in proverbial matters which have no cause or construes reputable factious facts, of an uncountable measure like that of religion and ethics.

Can any proportion of reason, be estimated to following differential paths of seriousness relate to no cohesion (unless you want it too) of unity; like an insistent character it will not absolve its commonality or aspirant like insistence. And nowhere can any ordeal of ideals achieve a more higher homeostasis that it totally recounts in cordial matters of cooperation or association, like recounting of names that have cause; by first its insistence then by its association with its polarity in earnest seeking of reason. In any tantamount, there shall be a reputable act in justifying just how our relativity coexist with all matters and knowledge such that an absolving truly conduce our own nature in a reprievable appropriation to convict factual aspirations. Then the accumulation of relativity truly conflicts to the disassociation of an affluent justice in a palpably duality like reality's nominal prosperity of retributions complimentary. And in any reasoning applicability would be irrelevant in associating factors that appropriate a lucent ulterior of absolving to fictional characters that do not articulate a comportment of associating concepts, to the ulterior knowledge's, that try to associate with the amazement and drunkenness skillful planning and conciseness.

These different practice's cannot be more appealed or acquiesced to a diligent justification that truly, which neither relates or recants to by which it is comprising in actuality the conscience of expectation. And in all actuality can we approve the natural deviance by being acquired in tributary and resolute in assertiveness accepting colloquial.

Though just as time provides relativity can any justification act be good; for what good is in not acknowledging that any reprievable act conduce us to be unseen as not all is known and may well never be? In this postulating our disassociation with the affluent matter which truly neither apprize nor conceives of an absolute aberration; which so far is a disassociation in itself that neither acquires nor compels our own individuality by the accumulation of concepts by which is ill-reprievable and not heard. Possibly maybe the imaginative of conceptual material has its weight in the absolution of a precarious adventure through tumult of vicarious aberration of a mind we have; though such an ideal may well never be real, just as understandability may not be heard if one has no sense of ascension. Clearly through any ill-reprievable virtues can any convalescent concordance be received even in all actuality by how much time our accumulation of material be composed of, something not real; or the figment of any real plurality be ill-conceived or uncondensed such that our realities collide with affluent—aspirant verbatim—likely regularity can only arbitrate a nice necessity reputably toward relevance.

But shall we not control a natural plurality by a divisive accumulation that has neither a cause nor reputability because even in time we lose track of ourselves. Our repressive—singularity adduces with sustenance in characteristic features that absolutely acquire in confining a maxim—by which it is applied to the actualization of self. Properly, even in insistent nature of time can any singularity of affluence actuate the actual compositor of a relativity by which reason clearly inoculates and congruently absolves a progressive reality; by fragmenting our reality in idealistic rationale in actuality's time and conglomeration that neither cares to correct or assess confluent vagrancy? Importantly, our prospect like any ordeal in manner must assume nothing because we are clearly acting on the material by which it had no cause or justifying commonality that truly precludes to love an insistent nature. Positively, the affirming as it is known, in likeability by fragmented pieces of actualizing frank matters; like any cause that did not have any reception to an aberration which truly precludes loving and annulling reputable actions.

What idea do you measure your propensity or well-informed with such a degree of commonality that is already not been thought. Why must we interpret me as an insidious-stupid individual that has no intelligence as an exuberant king of authority. By which measures do you measure me? Do I not have just as much as you to understand and interpret the science's of knowledge; such that even in the measure of its justice's could any clearer decisive decision become as an accumulated endeavor that neither cared for justice or nature. By which claims are we making such that it's into an evolutionary process by which any divulgence would seriously supersede our accumulation. And can you provide me any knowledge of difference of the opposite effect that had not produced that by which it could be defined in reason? Can you show me someone who neither cares to know that true life exist nowhere because truthfully the earth is evil; and in any predilection that conclusively aspire to interrelate a cohesive bond to extra strenuous prodigality that any idealistic rationality has no place; and even in the fine figments of the sleeping reality, could any clearer reality be said to ever get a taste of its ideal. How about we throw all the bait and hooks off the boat and act like sharks so that way when someone ask if you are true belligerent man you can say I ran with the fishes; so clearly our own naming conclusively concludes that any reality could concisely capture the ever lucent characters of ordinance; like any care had a relative reality that even in its constants had no reputable absolutions, like a true dignitary needs words. And even in the dissolution of dissection can the influential process totally absorb the proper boundaries of the thought process of totally absolving with fragments of time that has no cause and never will because of mere impropriety. The justifications of the illusory can never conclude with an exact amount of just how revolutionary processes particularly articulate the absolute and the infinite planes of actuality which precludes our absolving in superior rights. Time now is like an actuality which completely does not care about absolution with relativity because an aspect that true knowledge rest in man; for what prospect have you that totally articulated to a resolute character that was truly dissolvable because of its involvement with the life of an ulterior-nominal realities like any reality is to be apprised of liberty and alterations of this reality that clearly aspires to associate common names and ground.

Where in fluidity can any focus be purported in an ever illusive affinity to actually archive materials for pondering aspirants and people to say there is no time, and there is nothing to exist except nothing, in perilous absolutions of relativity? This makes us inoculate a forceful material of prosperity, in theory, that can never be absolved like absorption of the ideal perpetuality that has never existed. This indignation should not acquiesce an articulation but have a resolute character in an aspiration that needs to have a cause and a care for a prosperous future, and euphoria that cares entirely to perpetuate a victory with a concise explication to intertwine reason with actuality. Conscientiously this offends our existence through ulterior motifs which these motifs completely dilute the figment of consciousness that truly diversifies the evolutionary process of conspiring to absolve the materialistic affixation that even, unclearly, wants us to thirst for prosperity's prominence of ulterior in life. This elementary principle needs to be examined as an indifference to arbitrate caustic because undeniably this convicts resolute consistencies in actuality that care to exist, and prosper the endeavor of artifice in individuality to the ever illusive relativity of conspiring to want more out of life. Though even arbitrating this articulating ideal the artifice must intrigue our reality by congressing in an ordeal of commonality in conferring that true dictation really impresses our mind to inquire into dynamic living. This is what we are to do about dynamic living is do that which we know but also do that which we do not know and in this unknown doing relativity of the world of rules will connect to an attribute of absolving our characteristic's that behold no promiscuity, but true reality in being cordial in inviting posterior perfection; like any ordeal this controls or reasons the associability as it truly confers that it is not in an idea to do that which has not been done but can and is done with a correlation that we do know even if we do not.

To be exuberantly sound in a perspiring originality of oneself has no lesser reasoning than an unforgettable causality of insight ; such that we resolve ourselves for contracting insights by being conducted in an imperial way to cosign aspirants, such as contemplation, to collide in respects to a superiority of mind state. In any insight it would not be not too concise to believe in one's own rhetoric, if in that rhetoric, we achieved mastication of prestige(reverence and perseverance of scripture, the gospel, and philosophy) such that the actuality of being this way of mastication aspires a hypnosis effect to project a full figure of our ideals in an effectiveness toward a natural reason of worldly matters and **conscientious prodigality.** But in any and this reasoning, we must conclude that the austere respect of living is like a consistency of imperatives representing our will, with an effort in conspiring to extenuate our effectiveness that concludes a dereliction to a true resonance that our reality is to be totally unapparent like any cause has any effect to want an end in post-modern society to fully see the wisdom of God. **Prosperously, our perception can concoct, with a resolution, to an association as perceptual reasoning collide with a conscientious reasoning that our dignitary aspires to idealistic relativities associatie for respectability in life as a form true prosperity and actuality.**

Truthfully our intentions should resemble logical reasoning in conspiring colleagues to expend and inquire into the likeminded ideals of perspectives of servitude ; such that these ideals associate a superior cause, and that this cause or reversible form of concise antics aspires, in us, to have relativity, in concordance to life, and in our own conscience our gestures be prudent and correct with humbleness and God. For this percept of God and humbleness has a respectability, and a true dignitary knows not to involve one's self in careless matters that we do not unconsciously make a mistake in not thinking truthfully because if we do not think then of the existential respectability that will not actualize our true selves as Solomon would have it. Timing in situations with this actualization in mind exerts restituted consciousness that conspires to speak wisely, for us, to interpret the meaning behind our existence and selves in a situation before it happens; such that this relativity of foreseeing is conclusively arbitrating, God's and our will in line with his, restitutions that involve placing precipice in conscientious forms of dialect and thought. Our destiny and transcendence from God is that we do not care but do, or the other idea is to inoculate our ability to be reprieved in the idea of an afterlife which has no time for self actualization; and this type of thinking can make our thoughts actuate by having kind of like a counselor in your mind and being double-minded, and these anomaly's are quite common, as sinners unconsciously interpret their own living in the world as theirs and not God's. With this ideal in mind there is reparations for transgressing the law and even if disbeliever has a truthful and reputable attribute this does not cause the causation in reality, or relativity, all it is idolatrous associations in thought. Figments of this though do relate to us believers but to the disbeliever associating thoughts to seem reasonable conduce them to believe that nowhere in their unconscious actions can their actions actuate an absolute life that that articulates their aspirations, if even in an artful and expressive form no way can they enlighten themselves to the truth of society and reason.

What about ideologies do we not understand; such that our interpretation of ideologies do not coincide with an absolute victory to our or others demeanor, or to the evolution of ordination; like being baptized, such that these ideologies are reputable before the lord and his glory of personal afterlife to come. Furthermore, In understanding these ideologies do we reason them without a will and the knowledge of the afterlife for a perpetuality as a successor that advises absolute vigor of ideologies understanding as they apply to us living fruitful lives? Secondly in these ideologies, am I like you or different in that I do not love, and care for an absolute victory of vigor of ideologies; or any propriety by which I do not like, such that my indignation is in jeopardy because both of us do not agree on all ideologies of knowledge; and this makes you higher than me in that you are fruitful for your own self and God's law of love is better and higher in you than me: here is parable Jesus spoke that speaks in this manner, "7And he put forth a parable to those which were bidden, when he marked how they chose out the chief rooms; saying unto them. 8When thou art bidden of any man to a wedding, sit not down in the highest room; lest a more honorable man than thou be bidden of him; 9And he that bade thee and him come and say to thee, Give this man place; and thou begin with shame to take the lowest room. 10But when thou art bidden, go and sit down in the lowest room; that when he that bade thee cometh, he may say unto thee, Friend, go up higher: then shalt thou have worship in the presence of them that sit at meat with thee.'[Luke 14:7-14:10]."

I do not say this on my own volition but of God's care for the ordinary transfiguration of his law, and I live life as it is secularly open to all, and organized in a plentiful of stacked boxes that only God can only touch. This is particularly my own beliefs about God and life because I feel as an infidel even though in the ideological concession of God's judgment I am saved by his son Jesus, which is commitment of great magnitude and provides God's transcendence of knowledge to endeavor you and me to profitable truths and wisdom. In this likeness we are different unconsciously in our suggestive attitude towards ideals and living in graceful ascension, of becoming more common, in providing ourselves with an utmost respect for God's and ideologies to appropriately want to live peaceful and godly lives. Clearly believing in God and ideologies are important and no one can tell us any different because true peace exist in the realm of the totally unapparent and unrealized knowledge of transcendence; because just as we learn life by dictating our actions or atone ourselves for the purification we produce holy exasperations and conclusions of righteousness in fluid and translucent subtleties that make life clear and honest. We must ask ourselves why do we live only to die and not justify our concerns as if they were God's or absolute figures of reason that have insight in the conundrum of hearing or appeasing our faculties that we access everyday and allows us to inquire into the human heart, mind, and soul by which God transcends a reasonable perspective if we believe in dreams and honesty. In these dreams and honesty our aberration for conclusive appearances in confounding qualities of reputability we associate with commonality of resolving perpetuality of God and ideologies; in this thinking it is as if we have no mind and if dreaming and honesty we must agree in Buddhist sense we do not have one. Everything exist as to please our mind states of nothingness; to be completely absolved by measures of reason and our insight convicts a reputability that always dissolves a restitution to our lives and nowhere is there a better place to be than in honesty and God's law. This makes our lives influential with precipice, that has no cause, time, or place, where we are nobody and in this actualizing we preclude to adulate the totalitarian attribution which is superior to all meaning or constituency, because our own minds have no cause other than surviving and this reputability is accentuated by prosperous measures that are recognizable to the human faculties and is resolving God, ideologies, honesty, dreams, actualities, and a restitution for surviving to want to cosign an individuality for the purpose of being influential toward people in general.

Though we as individual's of reputability need to have love for all family, friends, and people in a colloquial resolve to actuate an artifice that consoles the imaginative process of us perceiving a dutifulness of reason in congruence to living a fruitfully. This begs the question: "Why shall we hear but have no sight," in that finding this sight reverberates an evolution in a conundrum of precipice or reputability that allows us to have a good character to absolve our affixation in perpetuating the finer enlightenments of causality in our resolve to live peaceful lives. **Although, by a prosperous attitude we pursue a fruitful individuality that allows us to have a clear conscious like a blue sky of raining food to replenish and energize our being to a fluency of outstanding commitment to want to know truth and the truth of secrets. We must persist in an reality to conduce us to believe that a resolving of our affixation's in the metaphor of revolving doors to other worlds is to reincarnate ourselves to so many reality's of intrigue and prosperity.** To know we have nothing and to artificially atrophied a restitution that contracts a reversibility of parlance that extenuates an intelligible and common perpetuality and actuality is a corrective attitude as a means to endeavor on a concourse to have an influential resolve with nothing but happiness and peace that abides in all souls to want, seek, and have with nothing more than heaven on earth as **Confucianism** would have it.

I must concede I know nothing in part of my own individuality by which I am transcending or it could be god's love and I will never know until death. But clearly there is a respectability by which we inquire to accentuate with a immaterialist relativity that conspires to project how an idea or ideal can become just as real as if it could conduce us to exclaim holiness and no harm or resolute sounding imperfections can be deceive our reasoning if ideas or ideals which are not in line with God's reasoning. This thought process of reasoning with God derives from diligence, and knowledge, and, in fact, can conduce our own self-consciousness into aspirations that we never knew we had, and no other ideal can be higher, for how long can we meditate in this his consciousness? Always! **By now our conscious should confide in a resolute character, because by this resolute character prominent proponents of our naturalness in righteous thoughts gives a place of solstice and rest, and our hierarchy of access, in consciousness,**

propagates through this realities projection in compounding these idealistic fervors of resolute manners and consciousness; conspiring to these perceptual differences coincides, in us to believe, that we are purporting to accentuate the many realities of respectability in God that organizes ourselves to perpetuate to reprehensible thoughts and actions of life in this ever so blessed conscientious manner of progress. Our non-fiction of this God ideal of hope and respectability holds consequentially a good percept or precept that correlates in a manner of a training one in this certain thought or certain meaning because this faith represents higher ideals and breeds righteous dutifulness which is clear as air and has properties that resound with a sound a logical purpose that is equivocal to being obliged, through auspice means, to arrive at the same ideology God and politics that accentuates a causal way of appeal and concerting oneself in an adhesive strand of provocation and conscientious resolve to pontificate a sensible attitude but also know that true nature, and God resonates logical reasoning that will eventually have a total obeisance to a main goal to, "Never get found out."

Just exactly how are you to be perceived that an ordinary vexation would not ordinate through **any** reality which was not properly ascertained through using deducting logic; or have **any** reputability that evolves through condensation like it is heavenly and right is so much as we guide ourselves to want to do right. In this most beautiful religiosity: does it not resolve issues we have even though not by our own power? Would this affection of aberration and sincerity be seen as evidence which is a science or faith, and a dictation of either helping each other deduce character so fine and feel such that any fictional Person as Jesus standards come to life in our faculties aerate the earth? In these realities they do adulate by a prefix which sound by measures of affixing materialistic propriety, that clearly absolves and incarnates a refurnished world with just the right amount of cause so it is like any factual propriety that associatively adjust to fortune which is only in the right with apparel, the bible, and being pious; otherwise it just a concise computational rationality which is no more of a good thing than the reality which is still seen as good. Plainly and lastly, the idea is never to know, to always affix, but in a placement of attitude and conscientious beholding of some Samaritan atrophied I cannot help displace myself from the world that operates on money and glory;

that operates on a legal which is broke and is not reasonable, so what I am saying through the last statement is: be watchful with a close eye to the sky and God and this stupendous reality of living holy, righteously, and among others graciously will all be found just by following the bible and always educating oneself and taking to the right people for God's cause and will.

Impartiality in its sustenance is much exacerbated to a referendum cowardliness that has no good in the aftermath of trials. For you are like alone dove ascending to heaven because of its mere impurities on earth; and like dissidence can a plan or relativity aspirant of aberration be totally consumed and relented to behold and contract a restitute of inferiority. By which any standards, can we naturally atone the misfortunes of happening to the restituted manner, that has no outlook or cause to the oriented manner of causation; can we really love and have no resilience, can we really do anything we like because we feel like it, respectively within reason. What or anyone will convince you of the difference of humanity and interpersonal relations that succeed any commonality of resilience. And of any causation, of fragmented times, can you conclusively expire and interdict a restituted aftermath that had no resilience or cause that clearly did not aspire to do wrong and right and still be displeasing. Where are we going to find a home that neither displeases nor does not acquire resilience for manhood and godhood. Clearly our misfortunes are mistaken and in like any commonality shall our justice be ever consuming to inter-dispose of a relatively exacerbated result that had no cause and restituted manner of absence of trying to be good with God.

In any event our time is not an external apparition, but founding alliances in being an interpersonal resolution that that we are God's and all knowing; and in like any manner our feelings are not to aspire a restitution that had no cause or name to compose of fortunes, which neither here or there but of ill-reputability; saying murder is justified if in a lordship of a king if the murder has justifiable reason and seems safe enough to know the difference not to do it again or else punishment is done. I honestly do not think murder is wrong in strict sense of one being able justify their cause of action but even our President will not tell us what happens behind closed doors, and this is the extremist Muslims hate us; or why we have gangs that code of ethics and when you break them you are punished, same just a different type of government because this one is utterly dubious. But shall I impose a resilient aspiration, even unclear in concept, though ill-reposed or self-accepted that there was no trial by jury and I clearly had no naming of friends or common alliance to hold me together; but like unfortunate event I am not ill disposed to accept a philosophy which has no truth of apparent natures that neither absolve or require my name to be enunciated. Just as you like and love so shall I find my nature which I neither abhor or restitute to besiege to be of my own kin; I never found myself and even in this I am mistaken, and even in any commonality of acceptance would I be ill-disposed or unacquainted with common frugality in the acceptance of justice. But by any or which cause I am truly to be lost like a miner in a cave or an exacerbated referendum that had no cause for me because I was totally poor and not confounding in my restituted manner, that I did behold and love but only to lose it and never behold again. And in myself I am not like you and I will never be because my love is not of this world and any ill-reputability shall I succeed in the aspiration that not of my own but of the one who sent me.

Common as it would seem of our own dignity cannot totally aspire to be beheld and loved like anything cared or did not relent in the association of a time that neither is aspired to accept or divulge the nature by which it is affixed. I can no longer consume a natural existence of aspiration that neither involved me having a time of dereliction or unacquainted commonality of convalescence, which any true inter-personality would behold and succeed its judicature of an absolute variety of processes. But if any ideal be as affection or be its order of reason or out of like reason than I can neither abhor nor restitute that I decide and conger up consistence like any irresponsible actuality of acceptance would have me behold. I am clearly out of style, as liking to an existence of true imperialism that can be detracted and detected can any ill-manner recipient totally conclude that the ill-responsiveness articulate an infraction of convalescence.

It is all too cumbersome and clear, as any rationality shall have its fix, like in true harmony can we be so disposed to actuate any relativity that truly absolves and loves like any convalescence would have our time of truth. And I must be clear and stern that our truth of aberration with any true common cause of humanity has a desire and apprehension of resilience that concords and aspires to disassociate with the common occurrence of frugality and acceptance, just as how it is exposes the relevance of having no prospect to a contract. And even being inclusive would any part of our being be so insistent to constrict manners of an ill-recompense, just as how our persistence shall divulge could any blatant response to actuality actually resolve a common occurrence of **suffrage.** Though as we are what is being than any response that is derelict to an assortment of disassociation in actualities to reprove contrite necessaries in principle logic; like contestants of a time of attributive consolation, like the succulence of a good meal that arbitrates with any factions in reality that has truly become rational of any repose, and contesting our common occurrence can any reasonability interdict the percept of a thousand year mastication of peace and solstice. And as time has caused me to be reprehensible I too must atone for my character and logic for a natural essence has no cause or actuality toward reposing contrite reasoning; and just as time has caused much hardship so shall a dignitary of convalescence show the way of an enlightened people. With any ordeal of this magnitude or commonality comes as conscientious decision to aspirate a cognitive faculty of the preeminence of a secular and worldly horizon to properly assist in the future of prosperity and resolve so that harmony and tranquility relent with aspects towards uniformity in bondage to virtue and goodness.

Though I am also inclined to associate prosperity with common occurrence that has no reason of being, that have no godhood to truly be loved and aspired as a restitution which any conception of good can be totally transposed and interpreted to mean that our knowledge, tone, and character are the full fragments by which we are ourselves. **Still I will not relent, I will not hate, because I care for the common good, and like any noble want nothing more to be happy and appeased by a restituted manner that I have no cause for or totally resilient, if ever ending. And even in conception, can a true person love, like they had no name, like they cared because they loved not because it is their own interpretation; and like anyone I am at odds with myself, such that I behold and abdicate an acceptance like I was dying, and any response is totally unapparent and unworldly, and like any individual I am contesting that I do love and abhor that which I do not know for the mere commonality; that I am not here, that**

77

<u>I have no name, that I am nobody, and above that, in time, so shall I dissolute a common occurrence of good and wash out the bad.</u>

Though respectively, time, like any individual has its time and place because clearly I am stupid because I love not the common good by which it is bipartisan(biomechanical), why else shall a rarity of restitution be absolved and confounded to be believed that a common name or good cannot have as any respectable person, a good. Why else shall my time go unnoticed, is it because I unacquainted with a vernacular that neither has life or appearance of right because clearly our restituted manner does abhor that which it dislikes and even further of any not so sound relativity truly concoct a name by ordinances. In with the restitution of acceptance can any clear idea arrive that we have consoled the right function of illusory recompense, or any ill-mannered aspiring artist that has no actuality in catatonic resilience; like in times of peace and war could any aspiration completely depict, by firm measures, that we are beholding, in due time, a resilience like no other, and our cause could not be any greater by the restitution of man. Even as we unlike ourselves shall any responsibility **<u>Benedict</u>** in translucent terms by which any measure we have truly been imparted and excited to resolve because of true personality and absolution. And even in time of discord could any reality bestow a common good like it had no cause, like it was truly interpersonal in a confounding way that **<u>true superiority rest in the soul and not in intelligence.</u>**

Where shall any reason (prodigality) associate with any reality of coherence that did not truly compose itself with the attribution of affection; by which the infusion of exasperation arbitrates with a common artifice, like we have no name, yet we are totally disposed of locations in aberration, like we could not have any time or could not pragmatically interject precaution and passivism toward life and reason. If we inoculate ourselves with impacting our reason, coherently, in sounding to audiences as bipeds striving for absolution, such that our judicature of reason be resolved, then we must inoculate ourselves with a restitution too clearly absolve ourselves in any matter which stands to detract from our sense of naturalness and self. And the reasoning applicability to divisive aspirants need to be all be good and hard because in this reality interjecting any unsound reasoning will divulge unconnected pluralism in an infatuation of perceptive conscience, and in this the world there is no good. But if we are to completely absolve ourselves with naturalness and reason than any relevant adolescence must come from a commonality by which we absolve prefixes and acceptable consciousness from the masses, so that our time of mandate to heaven will come quickly and assertively. And the timing of heaven on earth is displaced in this naturalness by composing a restitution in manner that has a clear manner of consciousness to why, or when we orientate ourselves to interdict causalities of propriety and being in attitude of an acceptable plenitude for eternity and precipice in natural conclusive world of inevitability, the one, the only, true nature of reason and peace. Amen.

In obfuscation can any appropriation be indicted to a proverbial mind-log that can actually consistence as our framing of actualities conducing us to believe, "that any ill-rationality is unjustified on pretenses of provocation." If any actuality actuate our world to include the necessities in commonality that arbitrarily compose our senses to be totally explicated and sized to explicate by reasons of mere acceptance, could any rational conditions be obliged to behold an artful form of exasperation of life, reason, and God? And could any fictional masterpiece be totally articulated that our prospect not change as our thoughts and realities conspire to correlate with our conscience to not incline ourselves to accumulate such prospects that descend or ascend to these realities prosperity we have. Much in same sense truth can convict us to believe in associations of rationality by aspiring our time through congesting ill-refutability; that any time or rationality interdict, for us, to beseech life in idealism to believe in not acquired percepts. But in any of these percept's could, are, or the cause, or an attribution to be aspired to our perceptions of an unimaginable imagery to conduce our aspects to ordinate our correlation with the ideals that not all is real and no reasoning could applicably deny it. See, our time is in retrospect because in any naturalness could we objectify our prospects by which they impose, in us, to divulge a devotion to the direction of the unknown and unintelligible, yet have a sense of sensibility and all questions and answers be told because reliantly we are a resilient people and we all can have the same multitude and conscience as God would want us to have it.

Why, must our ordeals not affix time as it so real and profound that our occurrences do not fully compose the rationalities of conceptions we have that conspire us to believe that we do not aspire to orientate ourselves with the successive factors that offensively defend our **appeasement!** The rationality of this appeasement must be ensued to dictate our reasonable aspirations that any rationality in any form is an association conspiring us to love and aspire as God would have it for us to be good and professed in forming our ideals and appeasements; through the benediction of appeasement of finding our time as well as our ideologies that behold and aspire us to associate ourselves with any individuality or individual so that nothing did not ordinate, but our rationality and appeasement should suggest that as time goes on our individuality contest to the relations as common people and eventually one day universalism of people. It is just that our idealistic nature's must preclude to trust in our indulgences, such that they lead us not astray but that these prefixes inoculate our natural faculties which are so affixed in trying to divert from the wrong path of appeasement but in that appeasement let it be of God and good. This unorthodox of appropriations being God send devout Christians states: "That we do aspire with reason to know the ways by which our founding fathers did contest, that true godhood rest in the people, and if the people do not see, so shall no one else."

Our ideals of perfect edifice must concede in our evolutionary matter that precludes to evolve ourselves in the quality's as our rationality appertains to a usefulness in providing conscientious oration, by a priori influential consciousness. Even in our most indigenous ideals can this relativity totally elate, with a restitution, to provide an inoculation by properly understanding ourselves in obliqueness and sandier times of incomprehensible reason and conscience. And even though this does not reprove by divulging in our appellations of quantitative relevance, even our cause, of retribution should relativism actually acknowledge a plurality of successive appropriations in our lives by which is truant and alive. Even in this relativity of related associations our reasoning could not bring any clearer consciousness that obliges us to decide to form susceptible impunity, could we be anymore in a true precognition resolve, with resolute circumstances, that our perceptions be collective in perturbations in a more astute and actual nature than just blind sight in accepting pretenses which do not affix to causes which have no actual validity of consciousness, and understanding of the bible in the consciousness that the only real reality to life is truth which is inexplicably **reason.**

In our aspirant (soul) can any resilience provide any necessary tutelage by which any conscious being shall in the indictment of knowing be totally articulated towards refinement; that it affixes in our apparatus of resilience, or any affair that does not atone to the reliance on imperatives that depict in terms of naturalness; a commonality must invoke a restitution which invokes again an uncommon vernacular of compressing and compounding apparent questions, by our consciousness would have us question life and all its arbitrariness? So by any part of our being must totally acquire and itemize the deductive reasoning that attributes to the architecture for us to be enlightened and expend to an individuality that shines as the heavens open up, but this will never happen because people do not recognize me as the new son of God or a Sage.

To our appropriate forms envisioning related associative adulations of reasons in susceptibility we can and do not rebut but we make sense as it appeases the masses; with fair listening we can be judicatures to correlate our reasons with many susceptible obviousness's perturbed in graduating to an extent that even in times of our superlatives (reasons) resolve resourceful adulations of many Presbyterian affirmations that our individuality does conduce us to reprieve archaic slandering; this non-all or all-non reality pertains in being accepted by even if one does not know their language. This orderly relativity non-all and all-non is not inferior and should not be subsided in its form invoke referendums that actuate or rather cause our intelligence to involve our true nature to auspice much exclaiming in metaphorical senses to explicate conscientious reason and belief. This earnest or timeless of prosperity in reason and belief has an effect of naming the succinct factors that no reality can combine and destroy; but only that there is a fact, that any inclusion civility would appear with no sight to be seen yet seen in our subconsciousness. For there is no cause, no time, and a nothing that neither wants or likes the unknown but it is true even if unseen and hate that which is bad and do not what other than is good. Though this itself can never allows us to find or prove ourselves right because with our minds come no metaphysical standards at present themselves in a moment's notice. And just that we are convening to suggest or digest just realism with impairment to only know we do that which we do not know but that we do in the hopes that we do thus the idea of reason. [Biblical verse if needed]

In the event that there is imputable acclimations that supersede off every creature that our undeniable actions, mistake, and they contain a dilution of perception we must concede to perspire adulation toward a refinement of austere posterity. But even in our tantamount of posterity does aspiring perception acknowledge that we are without a doubt misconceived that there is not any possibility of future deprecation. Though in the inoculation what was lost becomes easily conceived as an effective result of imperial relevance that maintains a composition that in the evolution of processing acceptance of adulation, would this susceptibility be compromising? The purpose itself has a natural consistency like comparable trials of adulation by abiding by ultimate ideals that are transposed as relative association of variables that effectively convene together to provide sustenance and austere for most formidable consciences. Now, presenting an idealistic range of acceptance cooperatively perceives this in our own exegesis. This is a cause that is convicting a conclusion that deprecates in the taking back of what is relentlessly appearing to a projection of conspiring to expect time in circumstance to easiness of working or positive outlooks that have bilateral perceptions to exclaim ourselves reputable Christians or people. In this comparing a relativity such that our mind set contracting an invariable result, yet unclear though felt in an acceptation to consistent in probability so that eventually all relativity exacerbates referendums adulate precision of indefinite truancy.

In a cordial way, do we insight vigor that resolution would decide an assumption such that we are aspiring to readdress our aspirations in concourse toward efficacy. Containing in the idea means that a holy consistency appear as an affection comparing a superiority with resolute acceptance in a clear understanding of our reason and understanding precepts by which are a preamble to life's mysteries is consistent in a faith attitude to have. This is what I believe the problem is when we find ourselves detracted and afraid of assortment of numbers, in acquisition they dictate such that they act as a medium between multi-lingual and multidimensional words. I am under distressful conception that there is in life an aspect that has clarity yet is unlike any actual ideal that tries to behave as something of its life; it contradicts that there is impervious selves to detract from our perception of ourselves, and our reality thus then the idea of reasoning perceptively conspires to assist in the evolution of time.

Constantly the inquisition of finding retractable references has as an ideal that means to abide by self-projection, and relativity. We as humans suffice an association of relativity that decides am imperial residence that without clear perception has no meaning other than what is not known, and practiced.

Do we confide as a perceptual indifference to explicably pertain an action of unresolved exasperation that any decision relents, and appear real. In the ideal perception of our tantamount in exposition ascertains meaning to our individual conscience. I was wondering though does a reason have to be imperial to pertain of excess exegesis or reliant aspirants pertain to the exegesis that appeals and is reliant in affinity toward endlessness. But in this affection for commonality there must be a confounding ideal those ordinates a comparable that compromises a conception of a natural necessity. Hardly is time doing this because by the time we understand principles we are forgetful that we have said them. Reality is other than what we expect because resolutely our needs change, and are unmanageable to coerce our standpoint that extends perception I am however unclear that any individual necessity can exclaim an association that contradicts our excitement like an impervious subjection which we cannot hear but know without any immaterialism or material.

In business the thought process must be clear and deciding in that information and concise reasons are authoritative and leave room for subjection. What it does not do is explain a necessitude that exemplifies an associative subjection to reason beyond a doubt.

In contemplating business the ideal perception of authority relates to being assertive, conclusive, inquiring, and authoritative. I would not presume business is so different from life but that there must be extenuating circumstances why we are thinking in some sort of way that expresses we are cognizant of ideas, and self-expression. Like in a natural oratory are meanings must be clear, resound, and responsive. In the ideal that all life has a passivity that maintains reality, and expression of purposing expiation, or journey that one is naturally capable of being efficient and an asset. The reason that I maintain is assessing our minds our assets is to be conducive to the materials that maintain affection for cognizance in being clear, pertinent, and real toward all relativity that excites fervor.

Why would existence not believe that an ideal of resolute conviction in business not appease or coincide that logical placement extend expository prominence in conducting in a businesslike-mind to appertain resolute ideals and conscientious beliefs to maintain the business. This type of ethics provides subsequent idolization associatively as wants and an excessive ideals that no known natural plurality can exegesis, simply you cannot serve money and God at the same yet we have too.

Why must my need extenuate a circumstance that has no viable reason for wanting to be alive or exist because a natural reliance of factors examine that impose prediction. Through succinct factors our business perceptions of ideological concession examine me above conscience like an expository exemplification in existential circumstances upholding propitiation. In an ideal that explains existential circumstance our ideal resolution must coincide to extenuate a viable juxtaposition in confiding in the reality of reason. Though just as I am unreasonable can I subsume a natural exegesis that appropriates a decision that like debauching a severity irrespective by an ordinate of restitution in a true manner to explicate aspirations?

In the respect of ascertaining an ideal cataclysmic efficiency must conduce our decisions as the perception extends resolute. Without the ideal of conception our consistence conclusively maintains that all superiority coexist by Phantom Menace of sincerity of explication of a resilience of such forthcoming times exceed the explication of succeeding past acquiring imperial rise. The populace has as a precipitance an ideal connection to our associative properties that include being proficient in espousing an aspect in need that would appear lesser than apparel confounded in space. The precipitance of proposing resolutions in a perceptive state must aspire like the depiction that neither cared nor appeased a meaning that I was unresponsive or not depicting dilation in comparing the reasons for why it is. The individual conscience itself has a worth of long stalk elements in comparing that all relativity reacts an unfound intrigue in precipitating conscience of self. I would explicably want a perceiving disposition to merge into a world of unforgettable nothing that any individuality can possibly conceive. Perceptions in our idealistic nature relents that there is no need essential to confidence in that there is no need of predating oration as a form of intrigue. The reason of always conceding the proper respects of instituting relevance in abiding by a collective need of convicting interests or possibilities in enticing the rapture. Reality has in itself an appropriation to perforate an existential cause that our expense not coerce or explicate nature. I am not one to concede an ideal that had no meaning to conclusively to ascertain why reality of exemplification would expect a conscience to cooperatively conceive an acclimation of succinct factors that ostentatiously absolves figures of an imperial resound, but life has its causes and most are reasonable.

Predating a time that no expectable conclusion can be an inferior association have within it a percept that allows reception of explanation is exceptional in the aspiration that practicality exists as a reality. Possibly there like any reason contain in a supplement or back matter or deciding resolution that a perception in all ideals congruently measures in a thalamus of expense. An expression of compounding sentences such that an expository explication be dissolved from in an idea to mean that which cannot coincide to understanding is truant and receptive. Containing in themselves arbitrarily commit indulgence in not convicting or realistic depiction but in the denial of preeminence. Pluralistically, our infatuation is not intriguing if we are not in realistic reality of coinciding that life exists not as an extenuation but as an omen of unrelenting subsection of individuality. Complicating circumstantial evidence that neither connection nor folly was the ascertaining answer seen to maintain likelihood that all reality is relative.

What do we think of a natural influence pervading existential living applicable to recognizance of not aware or thinking consistently adding to fallacious ideologies that have a placement in expounding our fervor through translucent endeavors. I am at odds of a displacement that refers my own omniscience and tacit aberration for the fortitude to affix an endowing conception as ordeals probate to actualize a cognizant reason for masticating a dialect of fruitful reliance in asserting expression; then becomes incoherent to the catatonic consecrations that relate in any way to the exact precipice that makes life ample and supplementing our first thought that entirely relates in no way to what is to come. Yes, I am inadvertently saying life exist with exegesis because a pluralistic understanding can exacerbate an aspiration of such a magnitude that it infuses with collective meanings and ideas to be congruent to professing transcendence. One of these thoughts Kant would have it as a precognition or posteriori in affixing ideologies and our percepts to the compaction of flagrantly stipulating concocted relativity toward the progressing of many articulate regulations of the imperial army, yet am I right?

In justifying our causes they reprieve exhorting resolves to concordances that relate in such ways of self-seeking reproof for the formidable release that says: "Life is not all that is seen and in the event life exceeds, life will still prosper." So from this point I bid you a good farewell and happy day, morning, or night. God Bless.

REFERENCE PAGE